A SERVICE FOR PEOPLE

Origins and Development of the Personal Social Services
of Northern Ireland

Brian Caul and Stanley Herron

Published by **December Publications**
157 University Street, Belfast

© Brian Caul and Stanley Herron, 1992

ISBN 0 9517068 1 0

Printed by The Universities Press, Belfast

ACKNOWLEDGEMENTS

We received help and encouragement from many quarters. Our thanks are owed particularly to those who contributed from their experience of a life-time in social work. Thus we would like to dedicate the book principally to Miss Kay Forrest, former member of the Social Work Advisory Group, the tragic news of whose death reached us while the first edition of the book was in preparation.

We would also like to thank Miss Betty Hall, Mr Tom Shannon, Mr Les Andrews, Mr Edward Whiteside, Mr Victor McElfatrick, Sister Otteran, Reverend J Moore, Mrs Breidge Gadd.

In addition, we were able to benefit from current research on more detailed aspects such as John Beresford's thesis on the probation service and Michael Farrell's history of the Belfast Workhouse.

A special debt of gratitude is also owed to various members of staff in the University of Ulster, namely Mrs Sue Margrain (Research Officer), the Library and the typing staff for their unending co-operation, in particular Mrs Madeleine Lynch. Tony Feenan gave invaluable assistance with the photography.

The Public Records Office, Linenhall Library, the Ulster Museum and Belfast Central Library were more than helpful, particularly with regard to newspaper and photographic material. Dennis Barrett very kindly allowed us access to the unique cuttings book and minutes books which the former Belfast Voluntary Welfare Society maintained for many years.

Finally we would ask all those other people, too numerous to mention, who gave us their time and energy in obtaining information to accept our thanks.

Brian Caul
Stanley Herron

Opinions expressed in this publication are purely those of the authors and do not reflect in any way the official policies of any other body.

Foreword

This book represents the second edition of a text which was first published in 1980. The opportunity to revise it and bring it up to date after a ten year interval is particularly appropriate at a time when the further restructuring of health and personal social services in Northern Ireland within a general management framework marks in effect the demise of statutory social work. It could be argued that we are witnessing the end of an era which the book sets out to document, broadly the period from 1890 to 1990. There are three main purposes in this revised edition of the book:

> to give an account of relevant social services legislation in Ireland and, after 1971, in Northern Ireland. The legislation enabled the development of caring organizations, and debates preceding the enactments provided valuable evidence of contemporaneous issues;

> to offer a factual description of the development of social work and social services in Northern Ireland;

> whilst not primarily a social administration text, it attempts to discern certain patterns in the growth and decline of statutory social work and social services which illuminate the events that have taken place.

In the text, the term 'Personal Social Services' is used to include social work and social services in various settings: voluntary organisations and statutory social services (whether provided in hospitals, community, or the probation service).

Positive and negative factors have influenced the decision to produce the second edition of this book. We have been encouraged because of the demand for the first edition, which has been clearly demonstrated — it is on the required reading lists of all social work courses in Northern Ireland and appears to be meeting a real need. In fact it remains the only comprehensive narrative historical account of personal social services in Northern Ireland. On the other hand, the hopes which were expressed in the first edition that further research might take place concurrent with social service development, did not materialize. With the exception of John Ditch's "Social Policy in Northern Ireland 1939-1950" (1988, Avebury), there has been no published work which might be deemed to have superseded the present book. There is however continuing academic work in the form of theses for masters or doctoral degrees. We have drawn on this work with acknowledgements, because it is not readily available to the general public.

Contents

Chapter I
The Poor Law in Ireland 1800-1920   1

The First Poor Law • Voluntary Effort • Fever, Famine and Ferment • Social and Health Legislation • The Royal Commission on the Poor Law.

Chapter II
The Inter-war Years: Great Social Needs and Limited Resources   39

The New Structure of Government in Northern Ireland • Social Conditions at the Birth of Northern Ireland • Significant Developments in Social Services: Provisions for Children and Young Persons; The Growth of the Probation and After-care Service; Provision for Mental Health; Welfare of the Blind; The Birth of the Almoner Service; The Work of the Belfast Council of Social Welfare; The Formation of the Northern Ireland Council of Social Services.

Chapter III
Welfare and Bureaucracy   67

Social work and the Welfare State 1940-70 • Building a new foundation: The Dismantling of the Poor Law heritage and Development of Welfare Authorities, Medical Social Work and the Probation Service • Social Work Seeks an Identity: The Younghusband Committee and Expansion on Social Work Training • Diversification and De-centralization of Welfare Services; A New Adoption Act; Preventive Childcare; The Mental Health Act 1961 • Social Work in the Troubles: Phases of Civil Disturbances and Implications for Social Work • The Restructuring of the Social Services: The Health and Personal Social Services (Northern Ireland) Order 1972 • The Probation Service is Reviewed.

Chapter IV
'Personal' Social Services   119

Evaluation of Progress 1970-80 • The Extent of Poverty in Northern Ireland • Statistics Relating to Children and Young Persons at Risk and the Implications for Practice • The Needs of the Elderly in the Community and in Residential Care • The Mentally Handicapped and the Physically Handicapped • The Probation and After-care Service • The Potential Role of the Voluntary Organizations • The Fragmentation of Community Work.

Chapter V
The New Managerialism 1980-90   135

Stocktaking of Provisions for Persons in Need • The Implications of the Kincora Boys' Hostel Scandal • New and Proposed Adoption and Child Protection Legislation.

Chapter VI
The Need for Community Self-determination   163

Reflections on the Demise of Professional Social Work • The Challenge for Social Work Education • Direct Rule and its Consequences in Terms of Social Policy • Community Empowerment.

Bibliography   171

Photographs   175

Index   183

CHAPTER I
The Poor Law in Ireland 1800–1920

The First Poor Law

In writing about the beginnings of social legislation in Northern Ireland, the Act of Union of 1800, which brought Ireland under the control of Westminster, seems a convenient starting-point. However social legislation and social provision obviously existed before that date, and in reviewing the few measures which were taken before the nineteenth century, several themes emerge. Some of these themes indeed continued to colour later attitudes.

For instance there was a dilemma of how to separate out those who were poor because of age, infirmity or social circumstance, such as widows with children or children themselves, from the poor who appeared not to wish to support themselves preferring to live off others. The traditional way out of this dilemma was to make provisions so unpalatable that only the more destitute would avail themselves of them. Of course this sort of policy inevitably meant that the most needy also suffered.

The second problem concerned the relationship between England and Ireland where poverty was rampant. How could one adapt English provisions to a completely different set of circumstances, especially since there was not the means within the country to finance projects on the scale required? This problem was usually addressed in a negative fashion in the sense that the issue was ignored and inappropriate facilities were superimposed.

Finance constituted the third problem. Should a tax be levied on all ratepayers to finance projects or should one rely on charities, donations and subscriptions from the wealthy? In effect there was a heavy dependence on charity at this stage. Associated with this, there was the problem concerning what would now be called 'prevention'. Since poverty in Ireland existed on a massive scale there was concern to ensure that it did not continue to expand. In this respect short-term palliatives were seen to be the answer and indeed were the focus of what little social legislation was introduced before 1899. As George Nicholls, who was to be the initiator of the 1838 Poor Law (Ireland) Act put it:

> "The raising up and educating of poor children as Protestants and repression of vagabondism appear to be the objects chiefly sought to be attained by all these

Acts of Irish Parliament; and to these objects the relief of the infirm and destitute poor seem to be regarded as a matter altogether secondary and subordinate."[1]

Some of the legislation referred to by Nicholls is described below. In 1635 for instance the Irish Parliament had passed "an act for erecting Houses of Correction and for the punishment of rogues and vagabonds, sturdy beggars and other lewd and idle persons". The years 1703 and 1745 saw Acts which set up the first workhouses in Dublin and Cork respectively "for employing and maintaining the poor, punishing vagabonds, and providing for and educating foundling children". A further Act followed in 1765 for "erecting and establishing public infirmaries or hospitals in this Kingdom". In 1771 and 1772 there were attempts to deal with the problem of "eligibility" for assistance, with a tentative effort made to differentiate between groups of the poor. It was recognized that it could be detrimental to house "vagabonds and strolling beggars" in the same premises as children and so it was proposed that vagabonds should be sent to a "Bridewell" as a punishment for idleness. An Act was also passed in this period for "badging such poor as shall be found unable to support themselves by labour". Corporations were set up throughout the country composed of clergymen, members of Parliament, magistrates and charitable subscribers with the power to grant badges to the helpless poor and a licence to beg over a period of time. Authority was also given "to build hospitals to be called workhouses or houses of industry" — the latter term marking a change of attitude from the days of the original "houses of correction". Every man above fifteen years of age found begging without a badge was to be committed to the stocks and persistent offenders could ultimately be sent to the "Bridewell". The children of persons licensed to beg as well as fatherless and deserted children were to be placed, if under the age of eight years of age, in a Charter School Nursery. (Charter Schools had been set up by a Charter of George II in 1733 and administered by the Incorporated Society for Promoting English Protestant Schools in Ireland.) Children over the age of eight in these categories were apprenticed.

Consequently provision prior to 1800 was piecemeal and very dependent on voluntary effort. This was to continue to be the case after 1800 although a slightly different series of problems evolved.

a) To what extent, if any, could English legislation be applied to Ireland? Conditions in the two countries were quite different, with a degree of urbanisation taking place in England, while Ireland remained largely rural. Partly because of this, there were much better prospects for employment all the year round in England, whereas in Ireland, as we shall see, there were many migrant poor who travelled around seeking subsistence during the winter months.

b) Given the extent of the need in Ireland, how could the necessary facilities be financed? This raised the thorny issue of "absentee" landlords and the extent of their willingness to pay for the welfare of the poor of the parish.

c) Associated with this was the more ominous issue of the degree to which social welfare legislation could be used for social control. For example, by collecting all those without property into workhouses and gradually merging smaller holdings of land into larger units, the more monied land-owners could then take over these units and employ the able-bodied from the workhouses in them.

Notwithstanding, the Act of Union of 1800 had obviously given a new stimulus to the need to review provision for the poor in Ireland and a series of House of Commons Committees duly sat during the period from 1800 to 1830 to consider the problem. It is noteworthy that all of these committees came out against imposing English legislation on the different problems existing in Ireland. The 1804 Committee stated that "the adoption of a general system of provision for the poor of Ireland by way of a parish rate as in England, or in any similar manner, would be highly injurious to the country and would not produce any real or permanent advantage, even to the lower class of people who must be the object of such support". Following this, a Committee was set up in 1819 to investigate "the state of disease and condition of the labouring poor in Ireland", and described the prevalence of fever as a calamitous indication of general distress. The Committee commented that the disease is spread by "the migration through the country of numerous bodies of mendicant poor". In fact they recommended imaginative remedies such as public works schemes, including bog drainage, road-building, new fishing laws. The subsequent Committee considering "the condition of the labouring poor in Ireland" in 1823 developed this theme, mentioning the encouragement of fisheries, the erection of piers, the formation of harbours, the opening of mountain roads, the instruction of the peasantry in agriculture. In turn a further Committee looking at "The state of the poorer classes in Ireland" in 1830 recommended similar measures, specifying land reclamation, development of manufacturing industries and agricultural training as important priorities.

While these House of Commons Committees were deliberating, social legislation did not of course stand still. Among the most significant Acts were the following. In 1805 Dispensaries were established and this heralded the beginning of a General Practitioner service. From 1814-1818 Fever Hospitals became established and the first appointment of medical officers of Health were made. And in 1817 came the establishment of "lunatic asylums" in Ireland.

The scene was now set for a major review of social provision for the poor and this took place from 1830 onwards. By 1830 the operation of the Act for the Relief of the Poor (1601) in England was giving cause for concern and a Royal Commission was set up in 1832, chaired by Nassau Senior, to investigate the problem. The main difficulty in England was the large number of able-bodied casual labourers (for example, agricultural labourers) who worked for part of the year and subsisted "on the parish" for the remainder – an agreement which suited farmers very well in that poor relief operated almost as a kind of subsidy. To prevent this possible misuse, the English Royal Commission suggested two criteria. One was that the "condition of paupers should in no case be more favourable than the conditions of the lowest class subsisting on the fruits of their own industry". The second was that the offer of long-term employment in the workhouse could be an efficient test of eligibility for relief to ensure that these measures were carried out. The Poor Law Amendment Act (1834) was passed which, among other things, set up a body of Poor Law Commissioners for England and Wales.

As we have just seen, the system of poor relief in Ireland was also urgently in need of review and Westminster took the logical step of setting up a Royal Commission to investigate matters there also. The ten Commissioners appointed in 1833 were a distinguished body, which included the Protestant and Catholic Archbishops of Dublin. Although their report now appears as a humane, forward-looking document, based on extensive local inquiries, it should be remembered that their recommendations really summarized ideas which had already been proposed by the various House of Commons Committees mentioned above. The Commission estimated that there were in the order of 2,385,000 poor in Ireland. They recognized that with poverty on this scale, piecemeal measures were futile and they proposed three broad types of measure:

a) improvement of the resources of the country to provide work for as many as possible of the able-bodied;

b) assisted emigration for other able-bodies who might not be able to find work;

c) statutory provision for the sick, aged, infirm, lunatics and others incapable of work.

To develop the resources of the country the Commissioners proposed:

1 The reclamation of waste land.
2 Enforcement of drainage and fencing of land.
3 Increasing the funds of Boards of Works.
4 Substitution of healthy houses for unhealthy cabins.

5 Bringing agricultural instruction home to the doors of the peasantry.
6 Enlargement of leasing and charging powers to encourage land improvement.
7 Transfer of fiscal powers from Grand Juries to County Boards and "direct labour".
8 Authorizing Boards of Works to undertake any useful public works and to recover costs from local rates subject to the County Board.
9 To investigate the whole question of trade, manufacture, fisheries and mining.

It is worth mentioning that many of these proposals were, in fact, put into operation at a much later date. For example, the formation of local Drainage Boards in 1863; improvement of housing by the various Housing of Labourers Acts 1860 to 1906; agricultural training by the establishment in 1891 and 1899 of the Congested Districts Board and the Department of Agriculture and Technical Instruction; The Land Tenure Act of 1860; the establishment of "County Boards, the members of which should be chosen by those whom they shall be authorized to tax" by the Local Government (Ireland) Act 1898. Useful work undertaken by the Board of Works is illustrated by the later development of the railways.

Westminster was, of course, more interested in the group which the Commissioners left to the last (the sick, aged, infirm, lunatics and others incapable of work). They were also impatient to have concrete proposals which could be easily implemented and could not understand the length of time which the Commissioners were taking over their deliberations. Rather predictably, they rejected the Commissioners' wide-ranging and far-sighted proposals and dispatched Mr George Nicholls, a member of the English Poor Law Commission to carry out his own survey of the problem and report back.

> "As Mr Nicholls had never been in Ireland and as the age of guide-books and railways was in its infancy, he very prudently followed, with some short-cuts, the route taken by Mr Henry D Inglis the author of the most recent tour of Ireland. A reference to the maps in that book (2nd edition 1835) will show the itinerary of Mr Inglis, marked in red ink, and Mr Nicholls, in the first paragraph of his report ("a carefully prepared document of sixty pages in length octavo") mentions in their order the towns through which he passed." [2]

Nicholls' conclusion also was predictable: "The governing principle to be observed is that the poor law of Ireland should assimilate as nearly as possible to that established in England." The Government accepted his report and asked him to draft legislation which eventually appeared as the Irish Poor Law 1838. The country was divided into 130 "unions" (increased in 1850 to 163), and each Union was to have a workhouse. In each Union a "Board of Guardians" was constituted to levy a compulsory rate to finance the administration of poor relief. With regard to the granting of relief this was to be at the discretion of the guardians and consequently no poor person, however destitute, could be held to have a statutory right to relief. Relief was to be granted only in the workhouse; there was no outdoor relief. As for the implementation of the Act the Poor Law Commissioners for England and Wales had overall control.

How did these provisions affect Northern Ireland (or Ulster, as it then was)? Firstly, it should be remembered that much of Ulster (excluding Donegal) was demographically different from the rest of Ireland due to the "plantation" by mainly Scottish Protestants in the early seventeenth century. Secondly, possibly because of its geographical proximity to the increasingly industrialized North of England, industries found a footing there and certain urban centres, notably Belfast, developed rapidly between 1750 and 1850. Excluding Donegal, Ulster had 22 Unions and was by no means the most poverty-stricken area. The worst areas were in the South West and North West of Ireland. Table 1 shows the number of relieving officers in different unions.[3] Table 2 shows the extent of workhouse accommodation in 1846.

Provision for the Sick

As with provision for the poor, voluntary hospital facilities often pre-dated legislation. In 1766 the Irish Parliament had already passed "an Act for erecting and establishing public Infirmaries or Hospitals (in this Kingdom)". In Ulster, the Archbishop of Armagh, the Bishop of the Diocese and the rector of the parish were appointed as a body corporate for this purpose. In County Down the first meeting of Governors took place in April 1767 and premises were acquired for what was later to be Down Hospital. The new local infirmaries had no facilities for surgery, which were provided at County Infirmaries set up under the County Infirmaries (Ireland) Act of 1808. Similarly Dispensaries (the equivalent of the modern General Practitioner service) did not spread until the Hospitals (Ireland) Act of 1818.

Epidemics were not uncommon in Belfast, as one might expect of a port. In the 1641 epidemic more than 5,000 people died in four months. In the 1689 epidemic, 3,762 died in six months and it was partly as a preventive measure that the first general dispensary was opened in 1792. It made two types of provision: one for the sick poor in the poorhouse and another – quite progressive – for the sick labourer or artisan, to enable him to return to work and not become a burden on the community.

The Poor Law

TABLE 1 : Relieving Officers

	Union	Population 1841 **	Relieving Officers
1	Antrim	49,168	- *
2	Armagh	110,408	9
3	Ballyclare	26,020	3
4	Ballymena	74,022	6
5	Ballymoney	48,812	6
6	Banbridge	87,323	6
7	Belfast	100,992	4
8	Coleraine	52,704	6
9	Cookstown	46,455	5
10	Downpatrick	74,948	- *
11	Dungannon	70,000	6
12	Enniskillen	81,534	11
13	Larne	38,758	- *
14	Lisburn	75,444	- *
15	Londonderry	64,740	6
16	Lurgan	71,128	-
17	Magherafelt	80,816	5
18	Newry	95,541	7
19	Newtownards	60,165	4
20	Limavady	39,058	5
21	Omagh	69,099	7
22	Strabane	58,883	6

** 'population' refers to the population of the Union.

* still to be appointed.

Table 2 : Workhouse Accommodation in 1846

Population 1841	Accommodation Adults	Residence Adults	Accommodation Children	Residence Children
Ulster 2,362,132	16,920	6,179	11,280	7,365

In the workhouses, four categories of resident were distinguished: the **healthy**, the **sick**, **children** and **lunatics**.

In 1794 the first lying-in hospital was established at 25 Donegall Street, Belfast by "The Humane Female Society" to cater specifically for the needs of poor lying-in women. It was followed in 1797 by the opening of the Fever Hospital in Belfast.

1829 saw the establishment of the District Hospital for the Treatment of the Insane. Prior to the Lunacy Act the only provision for the lunatic poor of Ireland was one Asylum in Dublin and one in Cork. This Asylum serving Belfast was designed to hold 100 patients but this figure had risen to 300 by 1850. Separate legislative provision was made for the criminally insane by the Criminal Lunatics Act of 1845. Treatment of lunatics was based on non-restraint and treatment by 'moral' means, ie "constant occupation, considerate tenderness, punctual regularity and the most vigilant attention".[4]

Some further details are given in tables 3, 4, 5 and 6.

Services for groups other than the sick in the workhouse were less well developed but this was partly because of the strength of voluntary activity. The phenomenal growth and prosperity of Belfast from 1750 to 1850 has already been noted and the city's readiness to look after its more vulnerable citizens was partly a reflection of this prosperity.[5] Table 7 (page 10) shows the rapid growth in population and demonstrates that housing managed to keep pace, probably because of the preponderance of factory houses.

Municipal Government

The Act of Union among other things led to the establishment of municipal government in Irish cities and towns. Life Commissioners were appointed, with responsibility for paving, lighting and cleansing as well as other matters affecting the health, safety and comfort of the inhabitants. The kind of conditions with which they were faced can be seen indirectly from the legislation enacted; for example, this extract from the Act of 1800:

> "... every person who after the passing of this Act, shall at any time carry or remove any night soil or ordure, through or along any street, lane or place within the said town of Belfast between the hours of seven o'clock in the morning and ten o'clock at night, and every person who by day or night shall empty any night soil, ordure or filth from any sewer, privy or boghouse or shall throw from any door or window into the same any urine, ordure or filth ... shall pay the sum of twenty shillings."

Voluntary Effort

In 1795 the very forward-looking Belfast Charitable Society, founded in 1752, was accommodating 90 aged and infirm poor and 90 boys and girls in its newly erected Poor House, while at the same time distributing outdoor relief to 336 poor families. (It took another 50 years before the concept of outdoor relief gained acceptance throughout Ireland.)

TABLE 3 : Occupation in the Asylum

Males	Cultivating the ground, weaving, winding and warping. Making and repairing shoes, pumping water, tailoring, smith-work, painting, basket-making.
Females	Spinning, knitting, making and repairing clothing, bedding, etc. Embroidering, quilting, washing in laundry, assisting servants.

TABLE 4 : Causes of Insanity in Purdysburn 1850

Moral causes	Domestic misfortune, grief, apprehension relating to a future state; jealousy, loss of property, pride, poverty, remorse. Fright, fear of want, reverses. Religious excitement and enthusiasm. Disappointed affections, domestic quarrels, over-application to business, over-study. Irregular habits, remorse of conscience, seduction.
Physical causes	Abuse of mercury and other medicines, bodily debility, puerperal affections, intemperance, effects of fever, epilepsy, disease of the uterus, injury on the head, effect of cold, indigestion, paralysis, sedentary employment, severe beatings, want of employment, unknown or hereditary complaints.

TABLE 5 : Ages of Admissions to Purdysburn Hospital 1840-1850

Age	Number
20	98
20-30	305
30-40	286
40-50	273
50-60	150
60-70	56
70-80	9

TABLE 6 : Education of Admissions

Well educated	49
Can read and write	565
Read only	290
Uneducated	160

A Service for People

TABLE 7 : Population : Belfast (Ballymacarret * is sometimes given separately)

Year	Houses	Population	Persons Per Household
1660	150		
1685	450		
1757	1,779	8,549	4.8
(1781: Ballymacarrett)	(96)	(419)	(4.3)
1782	2,122	13,524	6.5
1784		15,000	
1791	3,386	19,528	6.0
(1791: Ballymacarrett)	(279)	(1,208)	(4.3)
1802	3,179	19,001	6.0
1807	3,514	22,095	6.3
1813	4,415	27,832	6.3
1821	5,494	37,277	6.8
1822	5,932	37,117	6.25
1831	8,710	53,737	6.20
(1831: Ballymacarrett)		(5,168)	
1841	12,875	75,308	6.0
1851	15,009	99,060	6.6
1852	17,156	115,924	6.7

*Ballymacarrett is a district in East Belfast which was to become the centre of the shipbuilding labour force.

That poverty was not a big problem in Belfast at the turn of the 18th Century can be gauged from the fact that from 1792 to 1794 the general dispensary had only 733 patients, while the lying-in hospital had fewer than 50 from 1794 to 1800. Between

TABLE 8 : Voluntary socities since 1800

1801	Blind Asylum or Industrial School (Burgess Entry off High Street, Belfast). Under the direction of a blind man, Dennis Maguire. Baskets, nets, cushions, maps, mats etc. were made.
1807	Belfast Repository for receiving and selling the work of poor women.
1820	Female Society for Clothing the Poor.
1821	Branch of the National Institute for the Deaf and Dumb.
1826	Society for the Relief of the Destitute Sick.
1831	School for the Instruction of the Deaf and Dumb opened in Donegall Street, Belfast.
1836	Institution for the Education of the Deaf, Dumb and Blind opened in College Street, Belfast.
1844	Deaf and Dumb Institution.

1800 and 1830, when it moved to new premises it catered for slightly more than 100. In the same years only about 34 poor women annually were "relieved".

Voluntary effort continued to thrive[a] as indicated in the opening of various establishments or organizations listed in Table 8.

This prosperity, set against the ravages caused by the successive potato famines in other parts of Ireland meant that Belfast served as a powerful magnet to large numbers of a migrant population. Equally of course, the combination of rapid growth and the absorption of a new population created many social problems.

1850–1920: Fever, Famine and Ferment

Nicholls and the Government of the day could not have foreseen the severe test to which the Poor Law was to be put in the ensuing years, particularly 1846 to 1848, the years of the potato famine, the effects of which are so graphically described in Cecil Woodham-Smith's *The Great Hunger*.[6] Between the censuses of 1841 and 1851 the population of Ireland decreased by an actual one and a half million, or almost 20%, but allowing for what would have been an otherwise normal growth rate this figure could have been as high as two and a half million. Over one million died of starvation, fever and dysentry, including 20% of those who emigrated. In July 1847 the number relieved under the Poor Law attained the maximum, and it was estimated that 3,020,172 people received separate rations.[7]

---

[a] "On October 29 1820, as the collection plate was passed round after the delivery of Dr Hanna's sermon in aid of the poor house a person unknown placed upon it two Bank of Ireland notes to the value of £1,000."

A Service for People

The years 1850-1920 were very largely the story of trying to make inadequate legislation and inadequate resources generally meet quite exceptional needs. The demand took the form of successive waves of poverty which depended mainly on the success or failure of the potato crop and it was not until later in the nineteenth century that some attempt was made at a basic restructuring of the legislation rather than repetitive patching up of the existing legislative machinery.

Quite apart from the famine, living conditions in Ireland in the 1850s were appalling. To give some idea, the censuses divided living accommodation into four classes:

IV   mud cabins having only one room (as depicted in photograph number 1)
III   a better description of cottage, still built of mud, but varying from two to four rooms and with windows
II   a good farmhouse, or in towns, a house in a small street having from five to nine rooms and windows
I   all houses of a better description than the preceding classes

TABLE 9 : Number of Fourth Class inhabited houses in Ulster

1841	1851	% Decrease
125,898	23,613	81

(For comparison, the decrease in Connaught was 74% Munster 69% Leinster 62%)

The relative superiority of living accommodation in Ulster is shown in Table 10.

TABLE 10 : % Proportion of Families Living in Class IV houses 1851

Leinster	26.5
Munster	32.3
Ulster	12.4
Connaught	26.6
Dublin City	48.9
Belfast	9.9

Although Belfast was by no means a black spot, the worst conditions rivalled those elsewhere, as the eye-witness accounts of Henry McCormac, a local physician, show:

"I have visited abodes in Belfast where there was no fire, nor utensil, nor food, nor bedding, a little sordid straw, now on the bare boards, now on the damp floor

… Open, untrapped sewers, with filthy stygian streams, emit during the hot months, emanations the most sickening. The more ancient dwellings of the labouring poor in narrow streets and entries, crowded with children, fouled with impurities, are alike discreditable to this rising place, as to the time in which we live."

"... The shameless filth and indecency of the workhouses, long lines of sick and dying children, smeared with each other's excretions."

"It may be years ago, in this bustling town of Belfast that I saw a child in the faint evening light, sitting on the lower step of an outer stair, in a court within a court. Its hair was foul and tangled, its attire and person were sordid. Looking closer I could discern that the neck glands were studded and swollen...

(Other children) are pale, dirt-stained malady-stricken, breathing an atmosphere replete with every repulsive impurity."

The limited efforts of charitable individuals are mentioned in contrast.

"In Gwyn's Asylum, Derry, the boys are provided with gymnastic apparatus and a garden and contrast favourably with the dirty, neglected children that swarm in streets of the adjacent city. The little ones of Cookstown were treated with peculiar humanity by the late Colonel Stewart. They had access to his beautiful grounds and gardens and were entirely bereft of the squalid, dreary aspect exhibited by the young inmates of workhouses generally." [8]

Given this scale of poverty, the Poor Law authorities were in no position to deal with the massive additional need created by the potato famine. Nevertheless, the basic principle of the Poor Law was adhered to: the test of eligibility for relief by offering admission to the workhouse. This was re-affirmed by the Temporary Relief Act of 1847 which stated that "no person in occupation of more than quarter of an acre of land could be deemed to be destitute and that it was not therefore lawful for the Guardians to relieve such person either in or out of the workhouse". (This "quarter acre" clause was repealed by the Poor Law Amendment Act 1862 in so far as it applied to relief in the workhouse.)

The years of famine were followed by periods of relative agricultural prosperity which encouraged small landowners to expand. Unfortunately, capital was not available and there was great reliance on credit. Another year of major distress (1880) left many in serious debt. The Government was caught in the dilemma of on the one hand providing relief, often through charitable organizations, and on the other hand contributing to the distress by having to enforce legal evictions. The Relief of Distress Acts 1880 for the first time set aside the basic Poor Law principle already referred to; outdoor relief could be extended to *all* classes of destitute poor in times of exceptional distress. Further distress in 1886 was reflected in the Poor Relief (Ireland) Act 1886 when once again outdoor relief to able-bodied and landowners became permissible.

A Service for People

The Local Government Board was empowered to authorize Boards of Guardians of any Union to administer outdoor relief in food or fuel for a limited time to poor persons under such conditions as they might see fit to prescribe.

These extensions of the Poor Law of course brought their own problems, in the form of a greatly increased scope for abuse. A commission was set up in 1887 and abuse does seem to have taken place. In some weeks as many as 48% of the whole population of some districts were relieved. There were huge increases in those receiving outdoor relief, from 926 in 1856 to 54,434 in 1885, excluding orphan and deserted children boarded out. These figures were in spite of the fact that the population had continued to decrease by more than a million during the same period.

The deficient harvest of 1890/91 again forced the Government's hand and led to a more radical reform (although one which had already been envisaged by the Irish Poor Law Commissioners some fifty years previously). The Congested Districts Boards Act 1891 sought to improve conditions in certain areas by encouraging new developments in:

> agriculture
> forestry
> breeding of livestock and poultry
> sale of seed potatoes and seed oats
> amalgamation of small holdings
> emigration
> migration
> fisheries
> weaving and spinning
> any other suitable industries.

The Railways (Ireland) Act 1891 gave scope to Boards of Works to provide employment schemes. These new measures were still insufficient to deal with the crisis of recurrent potato failure. 1894 was another bad year and the Relief of Distress Act had to be re-enacted for a further temporary period; and there were further potato failures in 1897/8 and 1905 and 1908.

It has already been illustrated that Belfast was relatively free of the worst conditions in other parts of Ireland. Its very prosperity acted as a magnet and the period 1850 to 1900 saw further unprecedented growth as indicated in Table 11.

TABLE 11: Proportion % of the Population not born in the area in which they are living

	1841	1851
Belfast	22.95	43.33

The mixture of an 'immigrant' population and low social standards could be expected to lead to trouble, as it did. The period is marked by a series of riots mainly in Belfast and Londonderry which bear a distinct resemblance to those of 1969 and following years. The first serious riots were in July 1857 and were mainly confined to conflict between Protestant and Catholic working class communities living in close proximity to each other in West Belfast.[9]

All the features of recent civil disturbances were there. There had been some residential mixing in the communities but before the riots there was progressive sectarianism and intimidation. (Described with a sense of irony by the Public Inquiry: "The removals were often kindly enough effected on both sides; friendly notices to quit were often given and the extreme penalty for non-compliancy — namely the wrecking of the house — was in many instances not resorted to until the lapse of some time after such notice".)[10]

There were further riots in Belfast in 1863 and, more serious, in Londonderry from July 1868 to 1869. Again the official account has the grotesque déjà vu of, as it were, a silent film of the events of Bloody Sunday 100 years before the event.

"When the Bogside people expressed their unwillingness to risk going out by Bishop's Gate, the constable urged them to go by Shipquay Street, which would be a considerable detour, but they objected, probably from an unwillingness to allow a triumph to their opponents. Shortly after, however, the crowd in Bishop Street rushed down in the direction of Shipquay Street... It was at this time that the firing from the constabulary took place... one man was seen to be lying on the flags perfectly still and another writhing backwards and forwards."

There were still further riots in Londonderry in November 1882, the occasion being a visit by the Lord Mayor of Dublin and a counter-demonstration by the Apprentice Boys. There were more serious riots in Belfast in 1872 and most particularly, 1886.[11] The precipitating incident on this occasion was a quarrel between a Protestant and a Catholic workman in a predominantly Catholic group working near the equally predominantly Protestant workforce of the Shipyard ('the Island men'). During the quarrel the Catholic workman was alleged to have said "neither he (Bleakley) nor any of his sort should get leave to work there or earn a loaf there or any other place". News of this incident reached the Shipyard and the following day an organized body of about 100 Island men left work and set on the much smaller Catholic work group "many of whom were said to have been old men and others quite young lads". They naturally took to their heels; a number of them sought to escape by taking to the River Lagan and swimming, others by pushing out in a raft and on pieces of timber. One young man, Curran, was drowned in the incident. Almost inevitably Curran's funeral was made the occasion of a demonstration by Catholic Home Rule supporters and the whole process of civil disturbances was once again set in motion.

That this sporadic rioting took place against a general background of relative social calm and prosperity is clear from odd comments in the public inquiry reports:

> "During the summer a number of school fêtes are held and it is the practice for the children to march from their schools to one or other of the railway stations from whence they are to start and on their return in the evening to march in a similar manner homewards. These excursions are usually accompanied by bands, while the children carry banners, bearing no party political emblems but in some instances inscribed with texts of Scripture. Certain of these processions on the return journey assume very large proportions, especially on a Saturday when the parents and friends of the youngsters, having got home from work early in the afternoon, naturally make a point of meeting them."

Indeed so prosperous was Belfast that by 1880 it was the third largest port in the United Kingdom, being exceeded only by London and Liverpool. It had the largest weaving factory, the largest shipping output, the largest tobacco factory and the largest ropeworks in the world. The linen industry experienced a continuing boom between 1850 and 1875, followed by a period of stagnation. Average wages doubled between these dates and their real value, in the period of falling prices, went up by 200%.[12]

However with the major issues to deal with in Ireland as a whole – famine, large-scale destitution, problems of social integration – a social legislation for the more vulnerable groups was relatively neglected. Nevertheless, there was progress, particularly in the question of making statutes compulsory, and, towards the end of the century, in restructuring the administrative arrangements. In spite of this, it still remained true that voluntary effort continued to play a major role.

Further Social and Health Legislation is Enacted

The Medical Charities Act 1851 for the first time set up a complete machinery for supplying domiciliary medical relief in all parts of the country. Hitherto the sick had been able to obtain medical relief only in workhouse hospitals, in County Infirmaries and as out-patients in numerous small Dispensaries created under the Act of 1805. But these Dispensaries were badly equipped voluntary institutions. Medical advice was given to all comers but the supply of medicines was small and the doctors paid domiciliary visits only to those patients who resided within a short distance of the Dispensaries.

The Local Government (Ireland) Act 1872 transferred to the new Local Government Board all the powers and duties of the Poor Law Commissioners. Prior to this, the Poor Law Amendment Act 1862 had already introduced new provisions for boarding-out children: "Whereas it has been found that mortality among infant children admitted into workhouses without their mothers is very large, and that in other respects the workhouses are not well suited in all cases for the care and nursing of such children during infancy... it shall be lawful for the Board of Guardians... to place any orphan or deserted child out of the workhouse if they shall think fit to do so, by placing such child out at nurse." An age limit of five years was set, although this could be extended to eight years. Other legislation which sought to improve the situation of children in deprived circumstances included:

The Illegitimate Children Act 1863 dealt with the recovery of the maintenance cost of children from the putative father. The Orphan and Deserted Children (Ireland) Act 1876 extended the age up to which children could be placed at nurse to 13 years. The Regulations accompanying this Act represent the first step in what later became Boarding-out Regulations with provisions about the duties of foster-parents: cleanliness (the child was to be "washed once at least every day"), shelter, food and clothing, medical attention, schooling, church attendance. The relieving officer was obliged to visit the child once at least in every month and to keep a written record of each visit.

The Pauper Children Acts 1898 and **1902** defined the classes of children eligible for boarding-out and left in the hands of the central authority the fixing of the age limit. Some idea of the effect of this legislation can be gained from the fact that in 1872 the number of children under 15 in the workhouse was 25.5% of the total residents. In 1902 it had dropped to 13.1%. The Poor Law Act 1899 imposed statutory obligations on Boards of Guardians to have children who had been adopted with their consent visited "at least twice in each year by some competent person appointed by them and if not satisfied by such reports they can withdraw the child". This visiting was to continue for three years after the child had been adopted. Under Acts passed in 1851, 1854 and 1853, Guardians would provide outfits and defray travelling expenses of pauper boys going to sea and under the Pauper Children (Ireland) Act of 1898 they could also pay the apprenticeship fees of orphan or deserted children over 15. The Guardians were constituted the Local Authority for enforcing the provisions of the Infant Life Protection Act 1904.

The Poor Afflicted Persons Relief (Ireland) Act 1878 specified the deaf and dumb and blind paupers as needing services. Other groups were idiotic (ie mentally subnormal) and imbecile (ie mentally ill) paupers. Section 9 of the Local Government (Ireland) Act

1898 required the County Council to provide and maintain accommodation for all the lunatic poor and the Guardians were to make no payment in respect of them.

The Importance of Voluntary Initiatives

Although statutory powers were in existence little provision was actually made and once again it was left to voluntary organizations to pioneer developments.

For example, in September 1867 three Sisters of the Good Shepherd arrived in Belfast from Limerick at the invitation of the Bishop of Down and Connor. At the outset they lived in Bankmore Street near the Belfast Gasworks, taking over from some Sisters of Mercy who had been looking after a group of girls there for some seven years. They provided care initially for about seventeen girls. However, within a very short period of time, two of the Sisters had died from typhus fever due to flooding by the polluted River Lagan. The Bankmore Street house had to be evacuated and a cottage was acquired in Ballynafeigh which at that time was a village two miles south-east of the city. Eventually a convent building was erected and the Sisters and girls moved in in October 1869.

Further building took place over the next few years and among the outstanding leaders of the Order was Mother Mary Ignatius who promoted a vigorous programme of training for the Sisters in "Social Sciences and Modern Social Work".

In May 1876, Dr Dorrian also brought the Sisters of Nazareth to Belfast and rented his own residence in Ballynafeigh to them. Their initial task was to establish a Home for the Elderly, Nazareth House, on the Ravenhill Road, Belfast. One of the first residents was, in fact, a Presbyterian lady who applied in 1876 following an advertisement in the local press. There were so many old people needing care that Mother St Basil, the leader of the Order went back to their headquarters in Hammersmith and sent more staff to help out. It is estimated that in the succeeding years the Order cared for nearly 5,000 old people and 4,500 children.

The Sisters of Nazareth were also entrusted by the Bishop of Derry with the running of 'Sunnyside' Home for the Poor. This was eventually extended in size and still caters for the elderly and children.

In 1899 this Caring Order purchased 'Fox Lodge' on the Ravenhill Road, Belfast, and renamed it 'Nazareth Lodge'. The objective in obtaining this accommodation was to provide personal care for many of their young boys who had up to this point been living alongside the elderly in Nazareth House. So began a tradition of caring which still continues up to the present in Northern Ireland. The Order was eventually to expand its facilities by opening St Joseph's Babies' Home in the same grounds and St Joseph's Termonbacca Children's Home in Londonderry.

The Belfast Women's Temperance Association played a significant part in making provision for adolescent girls during this period. Its members were active prison missionaries who ran the Prison Gate Mission and a "Home for Inebriate Women". A certain Mrs John Lowry who was involved in preventive work among girls in Belfast and came across much acute deprivation, resolved to start a residential home where "each child could develop physically, mentally and spiritually in a secure happy surrounding". Her aim was very much a Christian one to give all children in need spiritual security. A Home was eventually opened in Belfast with the help of voluntary subscriptions in 1882 and 20 children were admitted. Larger accommodation was taken over in 1886 and in the following year the new Home, Shamrock Lodge, was certified under the Industrial Schools Act. Eventually there were six "Victoria Voluntary Homes" in operation and until the Whiteabbey Sanatorium was opened, a shelter was erected for girls suffering from tuberculosis. (Although the Belfast Women's Temperance Association is now practically defunct, a hostel for working girls operated under its auspices until recent times and Schomberg House, a residential home in Belfast, provided for 20 children in the care of the Area Boards.)[13]

Offenders and Children in Trouble

Up to the mid-nineteenth century, methods of dealing with offenders and children beyond control could be said to have reflected mainly a concern to avenge the injured and a belief in strong deterrants. It was only in 1864 that transportation to the colonies was abolished after many thousands had been transported, mainly to America and Australia. Indeed capital punishment for petty theft was by no means unknown.

Gradually, however, legislation was being enacted in Ireland which was trying to make more constructive provision for children and young persons who had committed offences or who were in need of care and protection. In 1858 an Act was passed, reflecting similar legislation in Britain in 1854, authorizing the establishment of Reformatory Schools for "the training and reformation of older boys who had committed offences against the law".[14] Closely following this in 1868 (1857 in Britain), the Irish Industrial Schools Act provided for the setting up of Industrial Schools "for the rescue and care of younger boys who by reason of family circumstances or environment or company, were in danger of becoming delinquent".

St Patrick's Catholic Boys' Home in Belfast was to be among the first Industrial Schools in Ireland when it was certified in 1873 by the Lord Lieutenant of Ireland. It had initially been set up as a Boys' Home in 1862 in the centre of Belfast and became an Industrial School shortly after moving to new accommodation in Milltown on the outskirts of the city, where it was able to provide care for one hundred boys. This was to be the predecessor of St Patrick's Training School which still provides care for Catholic boys committed under a Training School Order by the Juvenile Courts of Northern Ireland.[15]

The new legislation also led to the founding in 1860 of Malone Reformatory, the earliest predecessor of the senior school of Rathgael Training School (the current Training School for Protestant young people in Northern Ireland). The reformatory was established through the efforts of some local philanthropists, who were also to provide the highly unusual origins of Rathgael Junior School. At this particular time, the Royal Navy went from wooden ships to iron and steam and it was one of their defunct ships, the *Gibraltar* which was acquired as a Training Ship, the first base for Industrial School inmates. This reflected a similar trend throughout Britain. A voluntary committee raised funds to equip it and after being certified under the Industrial Schools Act in 1872 she was eventually moored close to Belfast shipyards. Two other moorings had been tried but proved unsatisfactory because of exposure to rough weather in Belfast Lough! It soon became clear that the rigorous, demanding life was too much for the younger boys. Tuberculosis was rife and conditions on board really militated against proper health care. It was therefore resolved in 1882 that a school should be established on shore for boys under ten years old and Fox Lodge, the eventual site of Nazareth Lodge, was rented for a time. Originally granted a Certificate for 60 boys it was catering for 133 boys by 1897. Consequently the Committee decided to obtain a lease from Sir James Musgrave for a former model farm of 22 acres at Balmoral, Belfast, and the boys were transferred in that same year.

In the meantime, there had been a Royal Commission on Reformatories and Industrial Schools in Ireland in 1883 and among its conclusions was that training ships were rather more expensive than land schools. There was also evidence, it was felt, of an unacceptably high death rate on board the ship. Thus in 1899 the ship (which had since been re-titled *The Grampian*) was closed and all the boys were transferred to the newly formed Balmoral Industrial School.

As already stated, the 1858 Reformatory Schools Act saw the creation of Malone Reformatory School in 1860. Some statistics recorded at that time make interesting reading:

Weekly cost of food per boy	2/6½d
Hours of work on the Farm	6.00am – 8.00am
	9.00am – 1.00pm
	2.00pm – 5.00pm
School hours	6.00pm – 8.30pm

The training appears to have been mainly along agricultural and horticultural lines and "the moral and spiritual side of the boys' training was greatly emphasized".

Probation is Recognized in Law

In the wider British context, the law was beginning to indicate a change in outlook towards offenders and this was to have significant implications for services in Ireland. In 1879 the Summary Jurisdiction Act enabled courts to deal with trifling offences by binding people over to keep the peace and appear for sentence when called upon to do so. And in the London courts, the Temperance League of the Church of England and other religious groups appointed people to attend courts with a view to helping the poor and deprived who had come up against the law. This marked the birth of the Police Court Missionaries, founded on voluntary effort and religious enthusiasm and the forerunners of the modern probation service. Indeed in 1887 the word 'probation' was to be used in this sense for the first time in law in the Probation of First Offenders Act. Later in 1907 the Probation of Offenders Act was to empower courts to release offenders on recognizance to be supervised by a probation officer if they wished. Magistrates were also empowered to employ probation officers and many of the Police Court Missionaries provided the core of the new service. It will become clear later however that the progress maintained in Britain was not to be mirrored in Northern Ireland, which for a variety of reasons required a considerably longer time to develop a probation service of any real substance.

The Origins of the NSPCC and Dr Barnardo's

The general growing concern about the welfare of children in the second half of the nineteenth century was indicated in the establishment of such organizations as the National Society for the Prevention of Cruelty to Children. The origins of this Society were in fact to be found in New York. The immediate stimulus for the formation of the New York Society for the Prevention of Cruelty to Children had been the rescue of a severely ill-treated adopted girl by a woman missionary and officers of the New York Society for the Prevention of Cruelty to Animals! A certain J. F. Agnew was to visit New York and returned inspired to set up an equivalent Society in Liverpool in 1883. He was later to meet the Reverend Benjamin Waugh in London and the new London Society emerged in 1884. Eventually the first branch of the Society in Ulster was founded in Belfast in January 1891, with Benjamin Waugh in attendance. By the early 1900s, branches of the NSPCC had been established in Lisburn, Londonderry, Coleraine, Portadown and Enniskillen.[16]

A Service for People

During this latter half of the nineteenth century too, a young doctor, born in Dublin, of a cosmopolitan family, was to make his own contribution to the care of children. Having come to live in the East End of London while training at the London Hospital, Dr Barnardo quickly became aware of the appalling conditions in which thousands of young children lived in the side streets of the East End. Many children had only the gruesome prospect of the workhouse to look forward to if they were without parents, and Barnardo decided to try to improve such children's plight by providing shelter for them. An incident is quoted when he in fact discovered the dead body of a boy whom he had turned away the night before. It is said that his famous slogan "No destitute Child ever Refused Admission", resulted from this experience. His first Home, at No 10 Stepney Causeway, was opened in 1866.

In the ensuing years he developed facilities for both boys and girls, including his scheme of "Ever Open Doors", in various large city centres. These were organized as reception centres, the superintendent having the additional duty of 'enquiry officer'. In effect this meant that he followed up referrals and if residential care was needed as only a short-term measure, the family was received into the appropriate "Ever Open Door". On the other hand, if the family were clearly needing longer-term care they would be transferred via the London "Receiving Houses" to one of the other residential Homes now being established in different parts of the country. It appears however that Dr Barnardo was alert to some of the problems of long-term care in large institutions and he implemented a fostering scheme alongside his Homes. Another scheme was devised for assisting the mothers of illegitimate babies. This came to be known as the Auxiliary Boarding-Out Scheme, whereby the mother could maintain contact and keep direct responsibility for the child's upbringing by having the child fostered within easy travelling distance. There were rigidly enforced requirements with regard to regular visiting, and consistent payment of expenses. The penalty for failure to uphold these requirements was the immediate threat to withdraw the child from the foster-home.

In 1875, Dr Barnardo had carried out a survey of child care needs in Ireland and established that the greatest need existed in Belfast. It was not possible to offer any immediate relief, but in 1899 the first "Ever Open Door" was opened in Great Victoria Street, Belfast. In the period 1899-1905, 3,300 referrals were received and over 500 children were admitted.[b] Outdoor relief was also given through the free meals of this soup kitchen. As no long term residential Home existed in Ireland, children in need of long term care were transferred to Homes in England. This clearly had implications for children who still had any semblance of family ties as they could become totally detached and often did not return to Ireland. The practice continued after partition and the majority of children involved in transfers came from Northern Ireland.

(There was to be a major transformation as a result of the Second World War, when travel between any part of Ireland and Great Britain became very difficult. The Belfast "Ever Open Door" was evacuated to the old workhouse at Kilkeel in County Down as the first Branch Home taking up to 70 children. In 1946, a boarding-out officer was appointed in Northern Ireland for the first time. Further residential Homes were opened; Manor House in Ballycastle was purchased in 1947 and Macedon House, Whiteabbey in 1950.)[17]

Poverty and the North Belfast Mission

Some areas such as North Belfast provided inescapable evidence of the stark deprivation and poverty that existed at the turn of the century. And it was in such places that voluntary efforts, usually motivated by strong religious drives, had such an important role to play. The plight of so many of the people of North Belfast was to convince a certain Methodist clergyman, Reverend William Maguire, that the founding of a "North Belfast Mission" could do something to alleviate the widespread distress. In spite of some opposition, he was granted permission by the Methodist Conference and in 1898 was appointed Superintendent of the new Mission. He set about converting local church premises into a 'People's Hall' and started a 'Free Breakfast' service to the poor. Thomas Anderson in *These Fifty Years — the story of the North Belfast Mission* [18] described the Reverend Maguire thus:

> "... He was indeed a father to the youngsters of the slums. It was their privations which aroused his deepest compassion and often his flaming indignation. What a picture he made as he strode along the street, a string of barefooted youngsters pattering at his side and a tiny tot clinging to each hand, chattering away for all they were worth – Daddy Maguire they called him."

---

[b] The following is a statistical outline of the work undertaken by Dr Barnardo from the opening of the Belfast "Ever Open Door" in 1899 to the end of 1906, the year following the death of the Doctor.

Number of applications	3,316
Number admitted to EOD pending enquiry	2,030
Number permanently admitted to London Homes	526
Number restored to parents or 'friends'	581
Number sent to situations, recommended to other homes or supplied with clothing	975
Number assisted from Auxiliary Boarding-Out Fund	88
Number discharged at own request	434
Number of applications declined or fallen through	657
Number of cases personally investigated	2,792
Number of free lodgings given	29,781
Number of free meals given	89,345

The description has a very paternalistic ring to it, but there is no doubt that this man was held in high regard by local people for his courageous and, in its historical context, radical outlook.

The Birth of the Charity Organization Society

As the new century emerged, the City of Belfast was to witness yet another voluntary initiative which was rooted in the philosophy of Christian fellowship and which was to lay further significant paving-stones on the route to the statutory personal social services. In March 1903, at a meeting in Belfast, it was suggested that the group of interested people present should unite as an organization "for the uplifting of the community by the furtherance of social reform and civic purity". It was also felt that this organization might do a great deal to educate public opinion in favour of "progressive legislation". They later decided on the title "City of Belfast Christian Civic Union". Mr William Strain was one of its founders and went on to play a central role in its expansion and transformation. Among its early endeavours was the attempt to remove "the betting evil" in the community and they started the campaign to have the betting news obliterated from newspapers on public display in libraries! The terms of reference of the Civic Union were wide and they went on to act as a pressure group to control the exploitation of children in employment, and to promote the development of proper leisure facilities for children. Improvement of insanitary and overcrowded areas was also regarded as a priority, as was controlling "immoral literature" and "objectionable post-cards". Several conferences on social reform were initiated by them, and this growing dialogue was to lead to various significant and unforeseen developments. In November 1905, a certain Reverend Dr Purves contacted the Civic Union by letter requesting that they confer with the clergymen of Belfast to consider establishing a Charity Organization Society similar to those already existing in various British cities. This resulted in a meeting in Belfast YMCA in December 1905 with the object of forming the City of Belfast Charity Organization Society. Mr Strain acted as chairman and spoke of the "great stream of charity" in the city and how much had gone astray and to no good purpose. It was Dr Purves' view that a Charity Organization Society would enable "a system of co-operation between the charities and the Poor Law; and secure fitting investigation and action in all cases". He described this as the first step towards "intelligent help". A guest from Glasgow COS, Mr Strong, described it as "sympathy guided by knowledge" and "rehabilitation of the individual through encouragement in habits of independence, thrift and industry". He pointed out that there were already 80 COSs in England, 12 in Scotland and 170 in America.

In effect the Belfast Charity Organization Society commenced operations in 1906. It had been born out of the desire of interested civic dignitaries, clergymen and businessmen to relieve distress in a systematic but concerned way. It could also be argued that there were strong underlying assumptions that, in the sense of moral guardians of public money, they could and should try to differentiate between the "deserving" and the "undeserving poor".

A leader in the *Irish News* on 4 January 1908 also related the role of the COSs to the Poor Law inheritance in Ireland:

> "The society (Belfast Charity Organization Society), however, denounce 'indiscriminate charity'. Carlyle and Kingsley are quoted to indicate the damage to self-respect there is in giving a citizen assistance in the 'name' of charity or under the auspices of the Poor Law. We know all that, and we know the feelings of the poor. We agree, too, that on this very account, the argument of the Society is a striking condemnation of the English system of Poor Law introduced against the protests of an absolutely unanimous Ireland into this country. The Society, when it put it that way, must have been aware that had not Mr Nicholl's adaptation of the English system been adopted in 1838, native knowledge would have been brought to bear on the situation. When they consider the worthlessness of British legislation in this respect, too, after pondering over its utter failure in every other department of Irish life, Belfast citizens may not be unwilling to entertain the reflection which occupies the minds of the majority of their fellow-countrymen — that it is not yet too late to give Irish knowledge of Ireland an opportunity of devoting itself earnestly and effectively to the solution of Irish problems".

The COS gradually established itself in Belfast and its progress was monitored in another leader, on this occasion in *The Whig* on 12 December 1913:

> "The Society can claim to have fulfilled its object of encouraging co-operation and wise action in all kinds of social reform work, and has done admirable service in clearing up the confused ideas that exist on the question of doling out charity. It has shown that to relieve those in distress is a task that demands intelligence quite as much as sympathy and by good administration has made the shillings given to it go farther than the pounds of careless givers who rely on their hearts rather than their heads."

In March 1919, it was decided to incorporate the Belfast COS into the newly created Belfast Council of Social Welfare. The work and traditions of the COS were to be carried on in a special case committee, the brief of which was to organize charitable effort so that "the charity of the City may be administered wisely and effectively". It was also to continue to seek co-operation between agencies and deal with cases of poverty, carefully "investigating these cases, and securing "fitting treatment".

> "It seeks to educate the community in the right methods of charity and endeavours to obtain for the poor the thoughtful help of all classes."[19]

The Poor Law Commissions of Enquiry

It is clear from these developments that voluntary effort was still carrying the main burden of welfare services and doing so very capably and imaginatively if at times on the basis of complex motivation and dubious assumptions. Although statutory provisions were there, there had been so many piecemeal amendments in the Poor Law that the situation was chaotic. The time was therefore ripe for a major review of the whole system. It might be thought that Westminster would have learnt its lesson from the experience of the 1838 Poor Law but, incredibly, the Commissions which reported between 1900 and 1910 repeated in almost identical detail the mistakes which had been made in the earlier legislation.

Again there were two separate Commissions of Inquiry. The 1906 Report of the Poor Law Reform Commission (Ireland) was a clear, humane document based on extensive local inquiries and not afraid to make explicit and to castigate earlier mistakes, particularly those made in 1838.

It began with a caustic critique of Nicholl's Poor Law Commission — ground which has already been covered here. It then considered the functions of workhouses and pointed out that, over a period of time they had come to serve several different purposes, some of them incompatible with the maintenance of proper standards.

At 11 March 1905 there were 109 Unions in Ireland, each with its own workhouse. The total number in workhouses on that census day was 45,195: the proportions are indicated in Table 12.

TABLE 12 : Numbers in workhouses in 1905.

One-third (14,491) were "sick"

One-third (14,380) were "aged and infirm"

One-twelfth (3,498) were "insane" and "epileptic"

One-seventh (5,900) were children

One-twentieth (2,129) were unmarried mothers.

The "able-bodied" (excluding unmarried mothers) amounted to only one tenth of the residents (4,667).

The report goes on to consider the needs of ten groups in the workhouse:
1. The sick
2. The aged and infirm
3. Lunatics
4. "Sane epileptics"
5. Unmarried mothers
6. Infants
7. Children between infancy and fifteen years of age
8. Casuals or "ins-and-outs"
9. Vagrants or tramps
10. Other able-bodied.

It is not too fanciful to see in this classification the seeds of what were later to become "Welfare Services" for certain vulnerable groups.

1. The Sick:
The Report recommended three types of hospital provision – County, District and Cottage Hospitals – partly based on existing provision but clearly detaching hospitals from all association with the workhouse.

(a) There were already in existence 34 County Infirmaries and 14 Fever and Infectious Hospitals. These were managed by Joint Committees formed under the Local Government (Ireland) Act 1898 and were maintained by grants from the County Councils, by voluntary subscription and by payments from patients. The County Infirmaries were to become "modern, well-equipped surgical hospitals in order that patients may in their own county receive most skilful professional and nursing attention". It might be mentioned in passing that several County Infirmaries in the North of Ireland were singled out for special praise. The new "County Hospital" at Omagh was specifically referred to as "an example of what we think a County Hospital ought on the whole to be". The County Hospital was also to be a focal point for nurse-training.

(b) To meet more local needs District Hospitals were also recommended.

(c) Finally, areas remote from County and District Hospitals were to be served by Cottage Hospitals manned by a dispensary doctor and complemented by a most imaginative system of district nursing.

2. The Infirm or Aged:
It was recommended that existing workhouses should be replaced by "almshouses". Alternatively "boarding-out" in what were now called "voluntary houses" was envisaged.

3. Lunatics and Idiots:
Proposals here were, perhaps, less progressive. Because of overcrowding in many District Lunatic Asylums it was not thought possible to arrange a mass transfer from workhouse into asylum. Instead it was proposed that existing workhouse property – which was to be vacated by the recommendation of the Report – could be adapted for this use.

4. Sane Epileptics:
Again, rather retrogressively, were to be assembled in two vacated workhouses.

5. Mothers of Illegitimate Children:
The numbers of unmarried mothers in workhouses were easily explicable by the moral attitudes of the time. The girl who had "fallen" was unlikely to be accepted into her family again.

Such moral attitudes also coloured the Report's recommendations which, for this group of residents, were mainly aimed at "reclaiming" young women who had had one illegitimate child and segregating her from the more "degraded" mothers who had become pregnant more than once.

They proposed two types of provision for those who had undergone "their first lapse":

(a) owned or managed by religious or philanthropic communities;
(b) managed by the Board of Guardians and with "specialist officers".

The "more depraved" were already being catered for by the Good Shepherd Convent in Belfast (and elsewhere) and, for Protestants, the Maternity Homes for first cases (also known as the Midnight Mission and subsequently Malone Place Nursing Home).

It is worth noting that the Commissioners "do not recommend the separation of any mother and infant until the child is weaned".

6. Infants:
Were divided into six groups -

a) illegitimate first-born infants
b) illegitimate infants other than first born
c) deserted infants
d) orphan infants
e) legitimate infants of ill-conducted parents
f) legitimate infants of respectable parents.

Again one can see in these categories early signs of the later distinction between "in need of care, protection or control".

a) The proposal for illegitimate first-born children was that they should remain with their mother at least for the first year.
b) Other illegitimate children were to be separated from their mothers after one year and boarded-out. It was suggested that more adequate provision for the unmarried mother would diminish the number of second and subsequent illegitimate pregnancies.
c and d) Deserted and orphaned children were to be cared for in the institutions set up for unmarried mothers with their first child. (The County or District Nursery.)
e) Legal action was proposed to remove the children from ill-conducted parents.
f) Finally, the sixth group (for example, widows with children) should be eligible for outdoor relief.

The recommendations also included far-sighted provisions for the boarding-out of children, although the reasons given were practical rather than emotional ones.

a) "The wish of the majority... is strongly in favour of it."
b) The general opinion was that institution-reared children, when put out in the world to work for themselves, were not "handy", as they had been too much used to having things done for them and owing to the natural division of labour in a large institution they had experience of only portions of work.
c) Not being used to small houses and to "common-place life" but to clock-work arrangements and to spacious rooms with suitable furniture and fittings, institution-reared children were found to be awkward and out of their element when placed among ordinary surroundings in the houses of the poor.
d) Children reared in institutions were thought to be not tough or hardy as children brought up in ordinary houses in the country.
e) Children in workhouses were frequently "contaminated and debased" by their parents and by their association with disreputable inmates.
f) There was a growing dearth of agricultural labourers.
g) "Boarding-out... is also the cheapest mode of rearing children."

The Commission was critical of the English method of 'inspecting' boarding-out children. "Every boy and girl at the time of inspection is undressed sufficiently for ascertaining whether the child's body and feet are clean and whether it is free from bruises of ill-treatment."

7. **Tramps**: (Casuals, vagrants, night-lodgers, ins-and-outs.)
It was estimated that there were 99 resident in Belfast workhouse at 11. 3. 1905. Two footnotes are of interest:

"Londonderry is included with ordinary unions because there is very little destitution in the city.

Ins-and-outs in Dublin are thought to be three times as numerous as in Belfast.")

The Commission recommended the setting up of our Labour-houses in Ireland where vagrants could be sent by order of a Court or Summary Jurisdiction.

The population of the Labour-houses would be:
   a) rural vagrants over 15;
   b) urban loafers over 15;
   c) mothers of two or more illegitimate children (whose children would have been removed from them and boarded-out);
   d) all parents who were unfit to be entrusted with the charge of their children, except mothers nursing infants. (They, it will be recalled, were to go to the General Nursery);
   e) able-bodied ex-soldiers, of whom there were quite a few;
   f) any able-bodied person failing to support themselves; one group they excluded were "itinerant musicians and entertainers". ("Few in Ireland would wish to interfere with genuine ballad-singers".)

8. **Other able-bodied:**
Some of these were in fact infirm and "should be treated accordingly". The main recommendation was that others should be eligible for outdoor relief.

The subdivision and dispersal of the workhouse population obviously had administrative implications. An early model of the future Hospital Management Committee emerged to manage hospitals, leaving Boards of Guardians to be responsible for outdoor relief, the boarding-out of children and the general welfare of the infirm and elderly.

The Report usefully summarized the new kinds of provision they proposed, with their functions.

1	County Hospital	Special surgical and medical cases
2	District Hospital	Acute surgical and medical cases
3	District Fever Hospital	Fever cases
4	County or Distict Consumptive Sanatorium	Pulmonary and other tubercular diseases
5	Almshouses	Handicapped by infirmity or old age

6	Auxiliary lunatic asylums	Chronic and harmless lunatics
7	Sane epileptic asylum	Sane epileptics
8	County or District Nursery	Girl mothers with first child infants
9	General Nursing	Mothers with second or subsequent illegitimate infants
10	Labour-house	Vagrants.

The thorny question of outdoor relief was discussed with mention of the possibility of an Old Age Pension Scheme. However, no definite proposals were made as regards the distribution of relief.

By this stage, the role of the relieving officer was taking on aspects which make it recognisable as an early form of social worker. The duties included:

> To receive all applications for relief made to him within his District and forthwith to examine into the circumstances of every case, by visiting the home of the applicant and by making all necessary inquiries into the state of health, the ability to work, the conditions, the family and the previous earnings and other means of such applicant and to report the result of such inquiries in the prescribed form to the Board of Guardians at their next Ordinary Meeting and also to visit male persons in receipt of outdoor relief whose relief is made necessary by temporary sickness at least once in each week and all other persons in receipt of outdoor relief at least once in each month.
>
> In every case of sudden and urgent necessity to afford such provisional relief to the destitute person... either by an order of admission to the workhouse or fever hospital provided there is room therein and by conveying any destitute poor person thereto; or by affording such poor person immediate and temporary relief in food, lodging, medicine or medical attendance until the next Ordinary Meeting of the Board of Guardians.
>
> Duly and punctually to dispense the weekly allowances of all poor persons belonging to his district. Such allowances to be given as far as possible at the home of the applicant and in no case to be paid at a house licensed for the sale of intoxicating drinks.
>
> In the case of every orphan or deserted child placed out at nurse or boarded-out placed under his supervision by the Board of Guardians:
>> to see the child safely given over in charge to the person whom the Guardians shall have selected for this purpose;
>>
>> to pay by advance or otherwise as the Guardians shall direct, but not less often than by monthly payments the sums granted by the Guardians for the maintenance of the child;

to cause the child to be vaccinated by the medical officer of the Dispensary District in which the place of residence shall be situate.

to visit such child once at least in each month and also when any special occasion shall arise for so visiting it and to report in writing immediately thereafter to the Board of Guardians on its health, cleanliness, and treatment;

to see that the child when of sufficient age to attend school attends the nearest National School or other public school and remains there during the ordinary school hours;

To keep a diary showing how he has been employed in the discharge of his duties on each day of the week.

The Commission Report of 1909

It might be thought that presented with such a comprehensive and forward-looking Report, which did full justice to mistakes made in the past, the British Government would have welcomed the opportunity to implement its recommendations. Instead, they made precisely the same mistake over again. The Poor Law in England, Scotland and Wales was due for review and Ireland was included even though this meant yet another Commission reporting in 1909 and without the weight of local opinion which the 1906 Commission had so carefully sought. This Report is a pale shadow of its immediate predecessor. After quite a lengthy historical preamble, it proceeded to a discussion of mainly administrative procedures without the 1906 Report's careful assessment of possible need. They proposed re-organization of Unions into County/County Borough Councils. Each Council was to appoint a statutory committee – the Public Assistance Authority – to manage all institutions and services connected with public assistance. The Authorities would work through a number of more local Public Assistance Committees.

One progressive aspect of the Report was the concept of Voluntary Aid Councils and Committees – a laudable attempt to co-ordinate voluntary effort alongside the new statutory provisions. The Report also delved more thoroughly into the question of outdoor relief, or as it was to be called, home assistance. Their proposals bear repeating:

1. "That outdoor relief be given only after thorough inquiry except in cases of sudden or urgent necessity.
2. That it should be adequate to the needs of those to whom it is given.
3. That persons so assisted should be subjected to supervision.
4. That, with a view to inquiry and supervision the case-paper system should be everywhere adopted.

5. That aged recipients should be periodically visited by officers of the Local Authority (who might be women) and by voluntary visitors.

6. That it should be a condition of out-relief that the recipients are living respectable lives in decent houses and that the Public Assistance Authority should have power to refuse relief in certain areas where living conditions are bad.

7. That power should be given to remove persons ... who are living in a state of neglect to an institution.

8. ... that widows should have special and individual attention.

9. Outdoor relief should not be granted, except in special cases, to any women deserted by their husbands during the first twelve months of desertion."

and so on.

Concerning the wider implications of outdoor relief the Commissioners were not in favour of extending the new English system of Labour Exchanges and Unemployment Insurance to Ireland, because Great Britain was essentially industrial in character and Ireland rural. They made no proposals in their place but simply suggested waiting to see how successfully the scheme operated in Great Britain.

Turning to the vulnerable groups which the 1906 Commission had so clearly defined, the 1909 Report largely echoed their recommendations.

1 For the able-bodied: they recommended Labour Colonies with "strict discipline and an open-air life". In addition one or two Compulsory Detention Colonies, under the supervision of the General Prisons' Board were also thought necessary.

2 The sick: all rate-supported institutions for the sick were to come under the control of the Public Assistance Authority.

3 Children: the Report adopted the 1906 Commission's recommendations but was cautious about wholesale boarding-out until its merits were more fully investigated and until one could be sure of the supply of adequate foster-parents. There was considerable emphasis on continuing supervision, even up to the age of 21. There was also a very thoughtful comment on the children of widowers.

4 Lunatics: the Report adopted the proposal of the 1906 Commission for Auxiliary Asylums.

The Minority Report

Possibly the most memorable feature of this unfortunate Report is the scathing Minority Report attached to it by Rev Wakefield, F Chandler, George Lansbury and Beatrice Webb. They rejected the Report's recommendations on the grounds:

a) that they effectively remove control of public services from the elected representatives;
b) that the whole health services is to remain a Poor Law function;
c) that no substitute is proposed for the abolished Unemployed Workman Act;
d) the retention of the 'quarter acre' eligibility clause for relief to the able-bodied.

The main moral to be drawn from the 1906 and 1909 Reports is that governments never learn from their mistakes. In spite of the thoroughness, humanity and foresight of the 1906 Commission; in spite of the 1909 Minority Report's warning of the precedent of 1838 which the 1906 Commission made so explicit, the 1909 Report sought to impose an inappropriate administrative structure on the sources so clearly described by the 1906 Commission as those best equipped to meet local needs. In practice, the recommendations of neither of these Commissions were legislated upon and services in 1920 remained in the same unsatisfactory state as they had been in 1900.

The 1908 Children Act

However, before proceeding to the birth and growth of Northern Ireland as a separate entity, it is important to take account of one piece of British social legislation which was to have far-reaching effects in Ireland – the Children Act of 1908. As has been seen, various Acts had been introduced during the second half of the nineteenth century relating to children. Certain legislation like the Infant Life Protection Acts of 1872 and 1897 had as their objective the protection of the lives of children cared for by persons who were not their parents in privately made arrangements. The Poor Law legislation, including the Pauper Children (Ireland) Acts, was attempting to provide for those orphaned or deserted children whose relatives were either deceased or unable to care for them. Paralleling the birth of the NSPCC, the Prevention of Cruelty to and Protection of Children Act of 1889 was applied to Ireland as the first legal measure to provide for children who were living with their parents but who were in need of care and protection.

Following on from these measures, the Children Act of 1908 was passed, described by Eileen Evason as "a landmark in the development of policy in the United Kingdom".[20] She points out that it was even more significant for Northern Ireland because it was to remain the principal Act there until 1950. (The 1933 Children and

Young Persons Act was not adopted in Northern Ireland).

Part I of the Children Act 1908 consolidated and amended earlier legislation relating to child life protection. For instance it imposed a duty on persons caring for children under seven for reward to notify the Local Authority. The Local Authority was now given the duty to appoint inspectors and the powers to restrict numbers and remove children from unfit premises. With regard to care and protection, the Act made it an offence to wilfully assault, ill-treat, neglect or abandon a child or young person in a manner likely to cause suffering or injury to health. Neglect was defined as the failure to provide adequate food, clothing, medical aid or lodgings or failure to obtain these through the Poor Law.

There was however some concentration on the needs of the child in cases where a person had been convicted of or committed for trial for offences against children. The Courts were given the power to commit the child to the care of a relative or other "fit person". They were also empowered to send children under 14 to an industrial school if there was no parent or guardian, or lack of proper guardianship, or a parent unfit "by reason of criminal or drunken habits". Significantly too, supervision by probation officers was recorded as a possible supplementary requirement when a Fit Person Order was made in the courts.

Evason [21] nonetheless suggests that the failure to adopt the new provisions of the 1933 Act meant that "an approach concentrating on the offence of the parent rather than the needs of the child pervaded Northern Irish social policy for a much longer period".

It is also noteworthy that the 1908 Children Act is still the principal Act in relation to children and young persons in the Republic of Ireland.

On the international scene, Ireland was soon to be allowing many of its sons to die or be maimed on the battlefields of the First World War. An editorial in the inimitable style of *The Whig* (14 January 1915) revealed a sort of recognition of the urgent social needs that continued to press on the home front:

> "But preoccupied as we naturally are with the national needs created by the great struggle in which the country is involved, and in which, according to Lord Rosebery's telling phrase, we are locked with the enemy in a "death clutch", there are claims at our own doors which cannot be ignored. In spite of wider interests that clamour for recognition these days, the work of our charitable and benevolent agencies must go on, and their demands are at least as urgent as ever. "Business as usual" is an excellent motto for the times, but it is just as essential that there should be a general disposition to aim at "charity as usual"."

CHAPTER I
References

1 Nicholls, G (1853), *A History of the Irish Poor Law*, John Murray, London.
2 *Report of the Vice-regal Commisson on Poor Law Reform in Ireland*, (1906) Cmnd 3202, HMSO, London.
3 *Papers relating to proceedings for the relief of distress in Ireland*, fourth series, (1847) HMSO, London.
4 Malcolm, A G (1851), *The History of the General Hospital, Belfast and the other medical institutions of the town*, Belfast.
5 Ibid.
6 Woodham-Smith, C (1968), *The Great Hunger*, Hamish Hamilton, London.
7 *Royal Commission on the Poor Laws and Relief of Distress; Report on Ireland*, (1909) Cmnd 4630, HMSO, London.
8 McCormac, H (1853), *Moral Sanatory Economy*, London.
9 *Report of the Commissioners of Inquiry into the Origin and Character of the Riots in Belfast in 1852*, (1858) Cmnd 333, London.
10 *Report of the Belfast Riots Commissioners*, (1887) Cmnd 4925, HMSO, London.
11 Budge, J and O'Leary, C (1973), Belfast, *Approach to Crisis (1613 1970)*, McMullan.
12 Ibid.
13 Based on material supplied by F Alexander, President of the Management Committee of Victoria Voluntary Homes.
14 Kelly, R McF, *The Roots of Rathgael*.
15 Based on information in a booklet to commemorate the official opening of St Patrick's Training School on 10 September 1957.
16 Allan, A and Morton, A (1961), *This is Your Child*, Routledge and Kegan Paul, London.
17 Personal communication from Mr Les Andrews, former Divisional Children's Officer, Dr Barnardo's.
18 Anderson, T, *These Fifty Years; The Story of the North Belfast Mission*.
19 *Seventh Annual Report—Belfast Council of Social Welfare*, (1922).
20 Evason, E, Darby, J and Pearson, M (1976), *Social Need and Social Provision in Northern Ireland*, New University of Ulster, Coleraine.
21 Ibid.

Chapter I – Appendix
Summary of Major Social Legislation

1635	Act for Erecting Houses of Correction.
1703	Workhouse (Dublin) Act.
1715	Act for Apprenticing Helpless Children.
1735	Workhouse (Cork) Act.
1765	Act for Erecting or Establishing Public Infirmaries or Hospitals.
1771	Orphaned and Abandoned Children Act.
1772	Relief of Destitute Adults Act.
1773	Beggars in Belfast Act.
1800	Act of Union.
1805	County Infirmaries (Ireland) Act.
1806	Hospitals and Infirmaries (Ireland) Act.
1807	Hospitals (Ireland) Act.
1817	Asylums for Lunatic Poor (Ireland) Act.
1818	Hospitals (Ireland) Act.
1821	Lunacy (Ireland) Act.
1822	Advances for Relief of Distress (Ireland) Act.
1825	Deserted Children (Ireland) Act.
1838	Poor Relief (Ireland) Act.
1845	Central Criminal Lunatic Asylum (Ireland) Act.
1846	Lunatic Asylums (Ireland) Act.
1847	Poor Relief (Ireland) Act.
1851	Poor Relief (Ireland) Act.
1858	Reformatory Schools (Ireland) Act.
1862	Poor Relief (Ireland) Act.
1863	Bastardy (Ireland) Act.
1868	Industrial Schools (Ireland) Act.
1872	Infant Life Protection Act.
1872	Local Government Board (Ireland) Act.
1876	Pauper Children (Ireland) Act.
1878	Public Health (Ireland) Act.
1878	Relief of Distressed Unions (Ireland) Act.
1891	Congested Districts Boards Act.
1894	Relief of Distress (Ireland) Act.
1897	Infant Life Protection Act.
1898	Pauper Children (Ireland) Act.
1898	Local Government (Ireland) Act.
1899	Poor Law
1902	Pauper Children (Ireland) Act.
1904	Prevention of Cruelty to Children Act.
1907	Probation of Offenders Act.
1908	Children Act.

CHAPTER II
The Inter-war Years: Great Social Needs and Limited Resources

After the First World War political decisions, as a result of the Irish Home Rule debate, were to lead to a fundamental transformation in Ireland. As a result of the Government of Ireland Act 1920, a peculiar form of devolution was imposed, which enabled the creation of Northern Irish and Southern Irish parliaments. These parliaments were given the power to unite if they wished. In the meantime, however, Dail Eireann having declared independence in the South in 1919, there was a period of negotiations between the Southern Irish and the English in London. Subsequently a Treaty emerged in December 1921 creating the Irish Free State with virtual financial autonomy and a sort of Dominion status. What of the attitudes of Northern Irish politicians to all this? The predominant Ulster Unionists appeared to be striking a position whereby they were prepared to accept a Parliament they did not really want as a sort of guarantee against involuntary alliance with the rest of Ireland. As a result the Parliament of Northern Ireland opened in June 1921 and by the end of the following year both Houses of Parliament had agreed to vote Northern Ireland out of the Irish Free State, a right given in the 1921 Treaty.

Thus Northern Ireland came into being, consisting of six counties as drawn up by a Boundaries Commission. Within the population of these six counties, two features were apparent. Firstly the people were split in terms of their attitudes about the links with Britain summed up by Oliver thus:

> "To the Protestants and Unionists, the new settlement represented a second best, a barely acceptable substitute for continued integration with Britain. To the Roman Catholics and Nationalists, it represented such a bitter disappointment, such a setback of their aspirations for a united Ireland that they could not find it in their hearts to give their loyalty to it. Both these attitudes persisted and deprived the system of the moral support it needed."[1]

Secondly there seemed to be a common lack of enthusiasm about the setting up of a separate Northern Irish Parliament with its limited financial powers. In fact Britain was to control about 88% of its revenue and 60% of its expenditure.[2]

The new structure of government in Northern Ireland was briefly as follows: Parliament consisted of the Sovereign, the Senate and the House of Commons. The Governor of Northern Ireland, in the Sovereign's name, could summon, prorogue and dissolve Parliament. The Senate was in the main elected by the House of Commons and in effect came to be permanently dominated by Ulster Unionists. The House of Commons had a term of five years and again Unionists held a dominant majority of the 52 seats. In addition Northern Ireland was enabled to send twelve Members of Parliament to the House of Commons at Westminster. As for the powers of the Northern Irish Parliament, these consisted of the making of laws in any matters exclusively related to Northern Ireland.

Dublin had been the centre for civil service administration in Ireland, so the new Northern Irish Government literally had to improvise at first, using temporary accommodation as it was available. The eventual seat of Government, Stormont, and the Royal Courts of Justice were not opened until 1932, and until then the House of Commons met in the Assembly College of the Presbyterian Church in Belfast. Lawrence[3] suggests that the actual functions given to the Ministries were largely determined by money available and the priorities for improvements as seen by the Government. For instance the Ministry of Home Affairs had a wide array of functions, including public health, prisons, reformatories, police, justice, Local Government services. Other departments also had responsibility for health services (ie Labour, Education, Agriculture) and this general fragmentation must have had a negative effect on the development of community services in the inter-war years. Two other issues also had a deep-seated influence on future developments. On the one hand, the chances of a constructive democratic debate within a political structure imposed on a split community were always minimal. In addition, Westminster was still in effect in overall influential control as all Acts passed there extended to Northern Ireland unless there was direct or implied exclusion.

The revenue available to the Northern Ireland Government came from two sources, local transferred taxes (representing about 10% of total revenue) and the reserved taxes collected at a uniform rate throughout the United Kingdom. Of great significance to policy decisions in Northern Ireland was the conclusion of the Colwyn Committee of 1925 which stated that contributions to Northern Ireland should be based on the difference between her revenue and her "actual and necessary expenditure", which was not to include any spending on services that did not exist in Britain or that were superior to services there. The Northern Ireland Government had decided in 1922 that it should pursue a step-by-step policy with Britain particularly in the area of cash social services (ie old age pensions, unemployment, insurance). It seems clear that this was politically motivated in the sense that Ulster workers would welcome parity of income and therefore feel more accepting of the political link with Britain.[4] However with 25% out of work by 1925 compared with 11% in Britain, it was inevitable that Britain, through the Unemployment Insurance Agreement of 1926, had to accept even greater financial responsibility. This also implied as a consequence that there had to be further restraints on the spending of the Northern Ireland Government in other areas.

Social conditions at the birth of Northern Ireland

Two extracts from the Annual Reports of the Belfast Council of Social Welfare set the scene:

> "Trade is still bad and unemployment great so that we have again a record of relief given, and in this, as for many years, we have been helped by the various naval, military and civil funds available for post-war distress. As we have stated in previous reports, we cannot supplement the Unemployment Grant except where there is sickness or other special distress, and then we have helped in whatever way was deemed most suitable to the needs of the family concerned."[5]

> "We have no hesitation in saying that the year under review was the worst we have experienced. Trade conditions are still very bad and many men and women who had Unemployment Grants are now out of benefit, and there is nothing for them but the workhouse, or to try to live on the small grant given in kind by the Guardians, as there is not work for all.

> The illness among the children of those who came was, in the majority of cases, caused by malnutrition, due to the extreme poverty of their parents through unemployment."[6]

Industrially it could be said that Ulster in 1921 had become relatively prosperous in comparison with the rest of Ireland, with its linen industry, shipyard engineering, ropeworks and tobacco factories. Agriculture, however, which was an essential source of livelihood was in a rather depressed state. And in general terms unemployment was much more severe and average income much lower than in the United Kingdom. Industrial depression was to hit Belfast hard, resulting in a rapid increase in the number of unemployed which remained at a staggeringly high level throughout the 1920s and 1930s. Particularly severe years were to be 1925, 1931 and 1938 when nearly 25% of the insured population of Northern Ireland were out of work, largely due to the decline in the shipbuilding, linen and textile industries.[7]

It is also clear that many social problems were inherited as a result of years of inadequate administration and misgovernment. For instance housing constituted a very serious social issue, exacerbated by the steady movement of the rural population into urban areas from the late nineteenth century, a tendency which continued, although at a slower rate after 1921. Table 13 shows the change which occurred between 1881 and 1927.

TABLE 13 : Changes in the urban and rural population.

	Population in Country Areas	Population in Urban Areas
1881	911,713	392,102
1927	602,190	677,569[8]

Between 1923 and 1939, 50,000 new houses were built but it was estimated by the Planning Advisory Board in 1944 that 100,000 more houses were required and 128,500 houses needed extensive or major repairs.

Many speeches in the early House of Commons debates reflected appreciation of the grossly neglected and underdeveloped state of services and some Ministers saw their mission clearly as not just keeping in pace with Great Britain but perhaps in some spheres establishing models that would be guiding lights to the rest of Europe. Their concern was reflected in the setting up in 1925 of a Departmental Commission on Local Government Administration whose mandate was to inquire into the whole machinery of local government. This covered all branches of local government administered by Town Commissioners, Rural and Urban District Councils, Boards of Guardians, County Councils, County Borough Councils. When its Report was presented in September 1927, it contained an historical review of the Poor Laws, County Infirmaries and Fever Hospitals, District Asylums, Public Health, Housing, County and Municipal Administration.[9]

The statistics regarding workhouses in 1924 reveal the need for serious and urgent reappraisal. In March 1924 there were 4,784 people in 27 workhouses in Ulster. This figure included 2,789 sick, 1,281 aged and infirm, 308 children and 200 "lunatics", "idiots", and epileptics.

A variety of reforms were proposed including abolition of the workhouses and Boards of Guardians and improvement in health and sanitary services. In fact the recommendations of the 1927 Report although influencing thinking considerably for the years ahead were to a large extent put to one side in terms of immediate action because of the Government's financial predicament.

The Report on the Administration of Local Government Services 1928/1929[10] further illustrated the extent of deprivation in Northern Ireland. Indoor relief over the previous five years had been given to 5,000 persons per year on average. Outdoor relief was administered to about 5,500. Special measures had been put into operation in Newry and Cookstown although it was only in Belfast that special relief on a large scale had been implemented.

In Belfast the Board of Guardians made an arrangement with the Corporation to employ men on "useful works", for instance, street works, and subsidized the wages given by the Corporation.

There were 320 children in workhouse accommodation and 332 boarded–out by the Board of Guardians under the Pauper Children (Ireland) Acts. The death statistics over the previous five years in the workhouses were recorded in Table 14.

TABLE 14 : Deaths of children in the workhouse

1925	2042
1926	2063
1927	2340
1928	2196
1929	2401

Table 15 lists the deaths of children in the workhouses under the age of 15 years:

TABLE 15 : Deaths of children under 15.

	1925	1926	1927	1928	1929
1 year and under	199	217	298	237	267
1 to 5 years	110	174	98	108	210
5 to 15 years	64	92	79	75	75
Total	373	483	475	420	552

With regard to health services, it is clear that Northern Ireland was suffering from fragmented administration and consequently underdeveloped services and again some of the statistics contained in this Report bear witness to that fact. The Poor Law Unions were divided into Dispensary Districts and the Guardians employed dispensary medical officers and midwives to cater for "the destitute and the indigent". Most of the hospital provision was in the form of workhouse infirmaries with private hospitals emerging if private initiative and funding were available. Poor Law Unions acted as rural sanitary districts with cities and towns providing urban sanitary authorities for public health services. Often it was the Poor Law dispensary doctor who was also used as the part-time medical officer of health. The 1928/1929 Report also recorded that seven District Hospitals were now operating, including the Waveney at Ballymena, the Route at Ballymoney and the Massereene at Antrim. It also stated that in several other Unions the Guardians were considering the question of converting their workhouse infirmaries into District Hospitals. The Report added that:

> "These Hospitals appear to be much appreciated by the residents... the accommodation which they provide for private patients especially meeting the needs of many persons who were reluctant to enter the old workhouse Infirmaries." [11]

The Report also recorded that the death rate in Northern Ireland for the period 1918—1927 had been an average of 16.3 per 1,000, which had reduced to 14.4 in 1928. (It is noteworthy that the average for the period 1922—1924 in other regions was 12.2 in England and Wales, 14.1 in Scotland, 14.6 in Eire).

A decline in the death rate caused by tuberculosis was recorded:

1918-27	1.80 average
1928	1.37 average

and this was attributed to the better sanitary conditions and special measures taken to combat the disease.

In general however, the lack of centralized reponsibility seems to have been a major factor in the comparatively underdeveloped health services, especially maternity and child welfare outside Belfast, and school medical services.

Poor Law services, which were to remain in Northern Ireland until 1948 in spite of all recommendations, continued to be financed through local rates and administered by local authorities. (In England and Wales the Boards of Guardians had been abolished by 1930 and their duties given to County Councils and Public Assistance Committees.) In Northern Ireland, as in England and Wales, it is fair to say that there was a reluctance on the part of Councils to make demands on the rate-payers, so that the Poor Law was not administered in any really comprehensive way. In fact the extent of Poor Law relief was variable and largely dependent on the funds available in the particular Union. The tensions caused by the great distress underlying this sorry state of affairs is vividly illustrated by Liam de Paor in *Divided Ulster*.[12]

Total Expenditure on Poor Relief

1924	1925	1926	1927	1928
£389,996	£409,769	£411,269	£448,240	£417,276

(Report on the Administration of Local Government Services 1928/1929 CMD 110).

The Inter-War Years

A statement from the 1929 Annual Report of the Belfast Council of Social Welfare reflects its preoccupation with providing bare necessities at this time.

"The organization of much needed efforts for the social well-being of the people and for the further co-ordination of existing efforts has become more difficult, so during the year the energies of the Council have been devoted to the relief of distress."[13]

The Report also recorded that 1,980 families received support. A great number of people were described as dependent on Poor Law Relief Schemes under which they obtained work for two or three days weekly. The BCSW also provided food and medicine for children whose parents could not afford it. As an illustration of the nature of the referrals received, the plight of one family was reported. In this case, the BCSW paid £4 8s to a man who was ill with tuberculosis and whose sickness benefit had been stopped because he had fallen into arrears with his insurance payments. The man's wife was crippled.

Michael Farrell in *The Poor Law and the Workhouse in Belfast 1838-1948* [14] also graphically describes the Outdoor Relief Strike of 1932 which arose out of the discontent fostered by the low rates of relief in Belfast. By 1932, 11,983 people were receiving outdoor relief and the combination of low rates and inquisitorial means testing had lead to widespread anger. In addition men were expected to do demanding labouring work as evidence of being deserving cases even if they were weak from hunger. The relief rates consisted of the following categories:

		per week
Married couple		
	with no children	8 shillings
	with one child	12 shillings
	each subsequent child	4 shillings up to a maximum of 24 shillings

Single men on work schemes got 3s 6d. This was in fact about half the amount made available in many of the English cities.

By the summer of 1932 Belfast's unemployed formed an Outdoor Relief Workers' Committee which called a strike of all men working on the labour (task) schemes. It was also arranged that three hundred single men would enter Belfast workhouse where it would cost more to maintain them (16s 1d per week) than they could get on outdoor relief. Various court cases resulted when this sudden growth in the number of "able-bodied paupers" led to noisy breaches of the archaic regulations.

In October, it was decided to stage a mass protest demonstration which would converge on the Belfast Workhouse from four different parts of the city — Falls, Shankill, East Belfast and North Belfast. The marches were banned by the Government, using the Civil Authorities (Special Powers) Act. In spite of this the marchers still assembled to be broken up by armed police and widespread violence and rioting resulted all over the City. Two people were to die from gunshot wounds and over thirty people were injured. As a result, the Government introduced a curfew in the Belfast area. The Outdoor Relief Workers' Committee was to call off the strike when, shortly afterwards, the Board of Guardians agreed to an increase in relief rates.

	per week
Married couple	
one or two children	20 shillings
three or four children	24 shillings
more than four children	32 shillings

All benefits, including those to single men and women would be paid in cash as opposed to food tickets.

SIGNIFICANT DEVELOPMENTS IN SOCIAL SERVICES

Children and Young Persons

Until the formation of the Northern Ireland State, there had been two Inspectors with responsibility for children boarded out from the workhouses throughout Ireland. Their catchment areas had been determined by a diagonal line drawn across the island! After 1921 the Children Act of 1908 and the Pauper Children (Ireland) Acts continued to be the principal guiding legislation for children in need of care. Within the newly formed Ministry of Home Affairs a designated Inspector continued to carry the inspectoral role within the new Northern Irish boundary. There was a requirement that the Unions had to send their returns to the Ministry notifying it of any placements made by them. The Inspector of the Ministry would then make contact and visit the boarded-out children on a regular basis. It was also part of her role to maintain contact with the workhouses and perhaps try to exert an influence in terms of having more children boarded out. She would also perhaps suggest suitable foster parents to the workhouse staff. The vision is inescapable of a conscientious lady hot-footing across the Province with the thick volume of Mooney's Compendium of Irish Poor Law under her arm. Judging from the high mortality rates in the workhouses, the sense of responsibility and concern to better the plight of the children was doubtless very high indeed.

In 1923 the Report of the Departmental Committee on Reformatory and Industrial Schools in Northern Ireland was issued.[15] At this time there were five Reformatories in Ireland: Malone Protestant Reformatory, Belfast; St Kevin's Reformatory, Glencree; St Couleth's Reformatory, Philipstown; High Park Reformatory, Dublin, and Limerick Reformatory. And these establishments provided care for 77 residents from Northern Ireland. Malone was the only separate Reformatory in Northern Ireland, although temporary placements were made at Shamrock Lodge Industrial School (Protestant girls), Milltown Industrial School (St Patrick's — Catholic boys), Whiteabbey Industrial School (Catholic girls).

Interestingly this Committee recommended strongly that the phrase "Training School" be adopted instead of "Reformatory", which, it was felt, had "an evil significance" attached to it which "the nature of the offences for which young persons have been committed has not always deserved". (In effect the term "training school" was only to be given to comprehensive legal recognition when the Children and Young Persons Act (NI) of 1950 came into force.)

Alongside the Reformatories, there were nine industrial schools operating in Northern Ireland, namely: Balmoral IS, Belfast (Protestant male); Hampton House IS, Belfast (Protestant female); Shamrock Lodge IS, Belfast (Protestant female); St Patrick's IS, Milltown IS, Belfast (Catholic female); Nazareth Lodge IS, Belfast (Catholic male); Sacred Heart IS, Whiteabbey (Catholic female); Middletown IS, Co Armagh (Catholic female); St Catherine's IS, Strabane, Co Tyrone (Catholic female); St Michael's IS, Lurgan, Co Armagh (Catholic mixed sex).

The position of Industrial Schools in Northern Ireland was described as precarious because the Probation of Offenders Act of 1908 had led to large numbers of children being placed under the care of probation officers who would otherwise have been committed to Industrial Schools. Table 16 gives details.

TABLE 16 : Belfast Petty Sessions District

Numbers of children placed under care of probation officers:

Year	Number
1911	10
1916	158
1917	166
1922	94

It was also stated in the Committee Report that the use of probation officers "has been productive of good results".

In fact the decline in committals to Industrial Schools in Belfast was striking, as indicated in Table 17.

TABLE 17 : Committals to Industrial schools in Belfast.

1908	254
1914	133
1920	37
1921	37
1922	21

There was a suggestion that police preoccupation with "the disturbed state of the City" had affected the priority given to juveniles. Be that as it may, Balmoral Industrial School nearly had to close because of the financial crisis which this decline in numbers produced, and many of the schools had to rely on trading profits for survival. The development of the probation service will be considered in its own right at a later stage in this chapter, but it is interesting to note that the relatively retarded development of the probation service was partly attributed in some quarters to the attitudes of Magistrates. It was suggested that some by-passed the use of probation officers and committed children to maintain the economic viability of the industrial schools!

At the time of this Committee Report, there was only one Borstal in existence in Ireland, at Clonmel in a disused prison. The Committee recommended that a Borstal for males should be established immediately in Northern Ireland but not one for females as the number of committals was too small to justify such an expenditure. It was also suggested that, if necessary, an existing building should be modified for the purpose. As a result, under the Malone Training School Act, Malone Reformatory was empowered in 1926 to take on the additional function of a male Borstal and was brought under the management of the Ministry of Home Affairs.

This Committee in many ways offered novel and enlightened arguments on such issues as a separate location for juvenile courts, the after-care of Industrial School children, and the special needs of child and young persons on remand. There is no clear evidence that these were acted on in any substantial way.

The year 1929 saw the start of the legal history of child adoption in Northern Ireland. An English Act had been passed in 1926 and an attempt had been made to introduce an amendment to allow English courts to make adoption orders in favour of people resident or domiciled in Northern Ireland but this was defeated in the Westminster Parliament. At the same time there did not appear to be any urgent public pressure for a similar Act to be passed in Northern Ireland. It was eventually introduced by the Attorney General, Sir Anthony Babington, in the following terms:

> "It follows the English measure that was passed in 1926, with certain adaptations and with a few amendments which have been inserted as a result of the working of the corresponding measure in Great Britain ... If this Bill becomes law, I believe that many persons, who are at present afraid to contract ties of affection for the children of others lest they be rudely broken, will be prepared to offer comfortable homes and happiness to children, who through the misfortunes of their parents, would otherwise have to depend upon charity, and would be condemned to a childhood barren of all pleasure and opportunity."[16]

Some queries were raised by other members as to the timing and necessity of such an Act. As to the timing one member commented that it was a time when people were about to revolt in the streets because of their economic circumstances, and seemed to imply that other matters should have priority. Babington responded that there had been pressure to introduce the measure from "a number of philanthropic societies". He also said that while it was difficult to obtain numbers of existing adoptions in the country, he felt the Bill was justified in terms of the number of adoptions which would take place in the future. Fundamental objections were raised by some members about the rights of natural parents and one member suggested that adoptions should be open to review after fourteen years. The Government resisted this as against the spirit of the Act.

When the Act was made law, there were differences from the English Act of 1926. In Northern Ireland, juvenile courts were not given the power to hear adoption applications. In addition there was an assumption that most hearings would take place in open courts and only in exceptional circumstances (such as a natural parent and spouse adopting an illegitimate child) would there be proceedings in camera. In actual practice, the hearings were heard in camera.

In spite of the code written into the Act that decisions in relation to adoption should be taken with regard to the welfare of the child there was subsequent evidence, similar to that identified in the Horsburgh Report in England in 1936, that advertising with financial inducements and profit motives on the part of the agencies were superseding concern with children's welfare. It was not until the Adoption of Children Act (NI) 1950 that further safeguards were built into the legislation.

In 1931 the Children (Amendment) Act (NI) came into force to amend and expand Part One of the Children Act 1908 and thus make further provision for the protection of child life. Sir Dawson Bates, the Minister of Home Affairs, introduced the Bill, stating that its aim was to carry into effect recommendations made by the

Departmental Committee on Local Government Administration with a view to strengthening the 1908 Act. Up to this point the Local Authority which was the Board of Guardians was notified after a child had been sent to a home. Notice would now be required at least 48 hours in advance of placement. There was concern about people acting as intermediaries between parents and potential substitute parents. As the Minister put it:

> "It is quite a common thing for children to be brought from various parts of Ireland to a railway station in Belfast and handed over to someone here to keep. And these children frequently become a charge on the rates until they come of age."[17]

In other words, Ulster had been experiencing the abuses of baby farming. It was thus felt that new legislation would "strengthen the hands" of the Board of Guardians in terms of much fuller information being required. Parental responsibility for contributions would now be subject to closer scrutiny. The Act also raised the age limit for the protection of children from 7 years to the current school leaving age of 14 years.

There was also concern about the numbers of mothers in employment, particularly in the Belfast and Londonderry areas, who were placing their children in unsupervised forms of day care. Henceforth it was to be a requirement that those people keeping children on a regular basis would need a permit from the Board of Guardians, which would fix the number of children to be kept. Child protection visitors were to be appointed who would have the power to inspect premises and sanctions could be withdrawn if premises were later found to be unsuitable.

In 1938 the Committee on the Protection and Welfare of the Young and the Treatment of Young Offenders (the Lynn Committee) produced its report.[18] Its main task had been to consider how far the changes brought about in the law of England and Wales by the Children and Young Persons Acts 1932 and 1933 (1932 and 1937 in Scotland) could suitably be applied to Northern Ireland.

The onset of the Second World War has been accepted as the main reason why the recommendations of the Lynn Committee were not immediately acted upon, although the question of lack of enthusiasm at a Government level is perhaps also pertinent. Be that as it may, the recommendations of this Committee are still interesting to reflect upon in retrospect.

The principal Act In Northern Ireland at this time was still the Children Act 1908. By comparison the consolidating Children and Young Persons Act of 1933 in England and Wales had brought about several significant advances. It had abolished the distinction between reformatory and industrial schools; it had set up special panels of magistrates to sit in Juvenile Courts; it had raised the age of criminal responsibility from 7 to 8 years and the maximum age in defining a young person from 16 to 17 years; the provisions for the protection of children and young persons in relation to criminal and summary proceedings were extended; and there were wider provisions made for the treatment of juvenile offenders and juveniles in need of care or protection.

Among its conclusions, the Lynn Committee recommended that the distinction between Reformatory and Industrial Schools be abolished. It suggested that there were several reasons to substantiate this. The existing differentiation, it was stated, was not logical as "neglected" children often came from even more deprived and immoral backgrounds and were often more "vicious-minded" — so it was not really a question of "tainting" innocents. There was in any event already a mixing of categories in such establishments as St Patrick's, Milltown, Shamrock Lodge and St Joseph's, Middletown. And perhaps, most fundamentally, an abolition of the distinction would be more in line with the principle of the new English legislation. The Committee also suggested that "Approved School" might be an acceptable blanket term for all relevant establishments.

Other recommendations included the adoption of regulations similar to the English Children and Young Persons (Boarding Out) Rules of 1933; that as in the 1933 Act, it should be Local Authorities in the main who should be deemed "fit persons" but they should be allowed to delegate their duties to Boards of Guardians (who already boarded out children under the Pauper Children (Ireland) Acts of 1898 and 1902); it was also concluded that improvements could be effected in regulations relating to children at nurse and in need of care and protection.

It was noted that as at February 1937 there were 361 children boarded out by the Boards of Guardians under the Pauper Children Acts. At the same time it was believed that some children were having to remain in the workhouses because of the lack of foster-homes, limited allowances and legal constraints (for instance a child could not be boarded out if his parent was an inmate of the workhouse). The Committee concluded emphatically that "the workhouse is far from being a suitable place to bring up children".

It is striking that some people giving evidence to the Committee suggested that a Tribunal or Committee should be appointed by the Education Authority in lieu of a Court to handle minor offences. However, the Lynn Committee felt that this was untenable as it would mean giving judicial powers to a non-judicial body. It was recommended that, with suitable reforms, the Juvenile Court was "the proper place for the hearing of all complaints against children and young persons". Additionally it was concluded that resident Magistrates should always be present as chairmen of juvenile courts, becoming "specialists". Alongside them, the Committee advocated that there should be other Magistrates, with "special qualifications" who could be known as

A Service for People

"Children's Guardians". (In many juvenile courts it had become practice for one resident Magistrate to sit alone).

In line with the 1993 English Act, the Committee called for an increase in the age of criminal responsibility from 7 years to 8 years, and recommended that the jurisdiction of the juvenile court be extended up to 17 years from 16 years.

Two further proposals, clearly in the interests of children, have still not been met; that juvenile courts be enabled to make Adoption Orders as under the 1926 Adoption of Children Act in England and Wales for the sake of greater convenience and cheapness of proceedings; and that the organizing of juvenile court accommodation, particularly waiting areas, should be geared to the rights to dignity and privacy of the juveniles and their families.

As part of its brief, the Lynn Committee also assessed the extent and nature of juvenile deliquency in Northern Ireland. It was reported that in the period 1934-36, there was an appreciable rise in the number of indictable offences involving children and young persons under 16 years:

1933	1934	1935	1936
238	439	557	600

However it was stated that the total number of juvenile offenders in relation to the United Kingdom was still small, so it was felt that there was no cause for alarm. Nonetheless several factors were outlined as having a bearing on Northern Irish delinquency. It was claimed that parents did not always exercise their responsiblities well enough. However, it was acknowledged that environmental factors were significant. For instance the housing in many parts of Northern Ireland was described as inadequate and the 1926 Census report was quoted to illustrate the point. This showed that 7,906 houses accommodated two families, while 1,141 accommodated three or more families. Unemployment and the lack of recreational facilities were also cited as important issues to be tackled. The question of the bad effect of the cinema was also looked at, but ruled out because of insufficient evidence! "Mental defectives" were felt to be particularly prone to anti-social conduct and there was a call from the Committee for better legislation and residential facilities to provide for such cases. A further recommendation was for the establishment of a "psychological clinic" along the lines of those already established in the United Kingdom, which could assist the courts in deciding upon the proper treatment of boys and girls, as well as having other remedial functions.[a]

---

[a] a child guidance centre was eventually opened in the grounds of the Royal Belfast Hospital for Sick Children in 1943.

In more general terms, the Committee called for a Central Advisory Committee to be established for Northern Ireland to advise on Juvenile welfare, Probation and After-Care, and co-ordination of the various organizations. It was pointed out that a model already existed in Scotland and there was scope too to form local councils or committees with duties which could include the promotion of voluntary social services.

The Growth of the Probation and Aftercare Service

When the 1907 Probation of Offenders Act came into force, some resident magistrates in Ulster, mainly in the Belfast area, acted largely on their own initiative and appointed a few part-time officers. Their functions still remained very akin to the original Court Missionaries described in the last chapter. When Northern Ireland came into existence in 1921, there were still relatively few around. Payment for their services was on a per capita basis per quarter for each probationer in their charge. J Beresford notes that even by 1936, total expenditure on Probation in Northern Ireland was £312 16s 6d.[19]

The English Probation system had been expanded and improved by the Criminal Justice Act of 1925. With this Act, appointment of probation officers became compulsory, probation areas were co-ordinated with Petty Sessions areas and local probation committees were established. These latter committees monitored the work of the officers, and became involved in appointments. Probation Rules relating to appointments, qualifications and working conditions were introduced and the Service duly began to expand. (And Scotland was to follow suit under the Probation of Offenders (Scotland) Act 1931.)

The whole administrative structure of the Northern Irish service differed from England where the Local Authorities were levied. Authorization of financial support in Northern Ireland was by the Ministry of Home Affairs, the exact source being the Petty Sessions Fines and Fees Account — apparently known also as the Dog Licences Fund!

Some guidelines did emerge in 1928 in the form of "Rules under the Probation of Offenders Act 1907". They were mainly concerned with the conditions of appointment of officers by Justices and the visiting requirements in relation to probationers. Nothing was offered which would bring the Service any more in line with the United Kingdom and the Rules appeared to be largely a repetition of elements of the 1907 Act.

Responsibility for appointing probation officers was given to the Ministry of Home Affairs under the Summary Jurisdiction and Criminal Justice Act (NI) 1935, although appointments were still only made on the recommendation of magistrates. It would appear that the Ministry had had to prod at least some Magistrates into action in previous years because of their reluctance to implement the 1907 Act. Certainly the statistics which appeared in the Lynn Committee Report in 1938 would raise many questions about the uneven development of the Service, as reflected in Table 18.

TABLE 18 : Numbers under Supervision of a probation officer	Year
146	1927
169	1928
180	1929
160	1930
170	1931
188	1932
152	1933
208	1934
267	1935

(The Committee did comment that the probation service appeared to produce successful results, although there was no information about behaviour after supervision.)

In 1938 there were ten probation officers employed in the Province, namely 5 in Belfast; 1 in Ballymena; 1 in Portglenone; 1 in the combined Petty Session Districts of Coleraine, Garvagh, Kilrea, Ballymoney, Bushmills and Portrush; 2 in the combined Districts of Londonderry, Dungiven, Donemana, Eglinton, Claudy and Limavady. The Belfast team included 3 women, 2 of whom were attached to the Royal Ulster Constabulary; 2 men one of whom was a Court Missionary and the other being an employee of the Catholic Discharged Prisoners Aid Society. All were employed on a part-time basis which meant that they needed some other occupation to survive, Probation work being in the words of one of the officers "only an auxiliary".

The Lynn Committee recommended that one or more probation officers should be present at all juvenile courts and the more important courts of Summary Jurisdiction. A further conclusion was that Probation "areas" should be set up each with its own Probation Committee; at least one male and one female officer should work in each area. Although the need for continued help from voluntary societies was recognized, it was emphasized that probation officers should be appointed on a full-time salaried basis and should be part of a public service. In relation to training needs, the Committee also quoted the sentiments of a previous English Department Committee (1936) which stated that: "Most of the work of a probation officer is similar to other kinds of social work and for this reason he ought to be well grounded in the principles and methods of modern social work for which ordinarily a diploma at a school of social science is the best preparation." Consequently the Committee urged that the Ministry of Home Affairs make arrangements for Northern Irish candidates to undergo training under the English Home Office Training Board Scheme which had been set up in 1930. With regard to facilities, there was a suggestion that, with the assistance of Local Authority contributions and Exchequer grants, Probation Hostels should be made available as a useful condition of residence in appropriate cases.

There is clearly no doubt that, had the Lynn Report been fully implemented, it would have advanced the probation service and much else besides to a level much closer to the United Kingdom Services. However with the preoccupation of the Second World War and perhaps apathy within the Ministry of Home Affairs, the probation service remained undernourished and still operating under the increasingly archaic Act of 1907.

Provision for Mental Health

In 1932 the Minister of Home Affairs with the help of the Resident Medical Superintendents of Belfast and Co Down Mental Hospitals was to introduce a Bill which was to have major significance in terms of attitudes to and provision for mental health in Northern Ireland — the Mental Treatment Bill. The aim of the Bill was "to amend the Lunacy (Ireland) Acts 1821 and 1901 and for other purposes connected therewith".

During the Second Reading, Sir Dawson Bates stated that:

"Although in England a comprehensive statute which in effect consolidated and brought up to date the law in regard to lunacy was passed in 1890 and a subsequent measure — the Mental Treatment Act — was passed in 1930, bringing certain valuable reforms into operation, lunacy law in Ireland for all practical purposes has remained unaltered since the passing of the Act of 1875."
[20]

"... As has been well said in the Report of the Royal Commission on Lunacy which was set up in 1926 "The keynote of the past has been detention, the keynote of the future should be prevention and treatment!"

Bates emphasized that major aims of the Bill were to combat prejudice and ignorance in the community and provide for the early treatment of sufferers.

Part I had as its object to enable cases of "incipient mental disease" to be treated in mental hospitals without any necessity for certification or the formality of judicial proceedings. In effect this seems to have been taken with very little alteration from the

English Act of 1930. Voluntary and temporary treatment would become possible and there would no longer be the requirement of a person being certified as of unsound mind. In the future public mental hospitals would be able to provide clinics at which out-patients could obtain advice and treatment and former hospital patients could return for support and treatment, thus hopefully preventing a recurrence of the illness.

Amendments were introduced in general law relating to mental disorder to try to bring Northern Ireland more in line with "the more modern English code". Thus certain terms were to be discontinued, namely: lunatic asylums were to be henceforth known as public mental hospitals. A lunatic was to be described as a person or patient of unsound mind. The adjective "poor" or "pauper" was to be substituted by the term "rate-aided".

There had hitherto been no limit to the period that a "certification of unsound mind" could remain in force. Now a Reception Order would be valid for one year only and then reviewed after two, three and five years.

The old licensing system at Quarter Sessions for private establishments under the Private Asylums Act of 1842 had come under criticism. This was now to be replaced by a system of registration by the Ministry acting on the advice of its own inspectorate.

There was to be scope in the future for the boarding out of patients in approved establishments.

While the House of Commons generally gave its approval to the new measure the Second Reading produced comments which are interesting whether specific to the Bill or in more general terms about the social condition prevailing at the time. For instance, Mr Healey, the Member for South Armagh, stated that: "You are adopting this measure here not because of any special need but because a similar measure was introduced in another place". He was in effect saying that he was not convinced of its urgency compared with the "interests of the agricultural classes" at that time.[21]
In the same debate Mr Connellan commented:

> "Hitherto we have slavishly followed the Imperial Parliament in many ways. Now we are slavishly following the Free State with regard to the description of mentally afflicted persons and the description of the institutions in which their diseases are administered to. I do not like this policy of imitation of either England or the Free State but so far as mitigating the stigma upon people who suffer from mental diseases and their relatives is concerned, I think everybody will welcome the departure from the expression 'lunatic' to that of mental patient." [22]

Welfare of the Blind

There were two Blind Persons Acts during this period, in 1920 and 1938. Under the 1920 Act, Councils of Counties and County Boroughs had been made responsible for the welfare of the blind but the only scheme that appeared to be of any substance was developed in Belfast. This included educational provision for 5 to 16 year olds; education and training of the adult blind; creating employment opportunities; supplementing wages and earnings; and making grants to residential facilities. The scheme was in effect worked mainly through the voluntary agencies on which Belfast Corporation was represented. These included: Belfast Society for Home Mission work among the Blind; The Ulster Society for Promoting the Education of the Deaf, Dumb and Blind; The Belfast Association for the Employment of the Industrious Blind; the Home for Female Roman Catholic Blind, Belfast (St Brigid's). The schemes as such received no Government grant aid, but capitation grants were paid to participating agencies.

One of the major implications arising from this legislation was that a register of blind people was already in existence in the various areas when the statutory services took up the reins after the war and indeed some of the welfare officers for the Blind continued their work under the auspices of the new welfare authorities.

The Birth of the Almoner Service

The very first almoner to be appointed in Britain joined the Royal Free Hospital in London in 1895 at the request of medical staff who felt that many of their patients were unable to carry out the treatment recommended. In fact they felt that treatment was largely a waste of time in those cases where patients' living standards were so low that they lacked sufficient food — Sr Charles Loch, the founder of the Charity Organization Society in England (later the Family Welfare Association) was asked to provide a social worker and it was from his staff that the first almoner went to work at the Royal Free Hospital with the object of offering help and advice and to refer to appropriate agencies for material help those patients who were found to be in need.

A significant stepping-stone on the way to an extensive Almoner Service was the decision of the Belfast Council of Social Welfare to establish the Belfast Hospitals' After-Care Committee, charged with the particular responsibility of providing aftercare for patients discharged from or attending hospitals in Belfast. A correspondent of the *Belfast Newsletter*, at the time of the First Annual General Meeting of the Belfast Hospitals' After-Care Committee on 26th November, 1936, attempted to put the scheme in perspective:

A Service for People

"The scheme is a new one, much needed in Belfast — a city in which there are five hospitals. But while treatment in these is the first essential in the case of accidents or illness, everyone realised that the aftercare of the patient is almost as important.

In many cities and towns in Great Britain, the hospitals provide trained almoners to attend to this. But in Belfast such difficulty is found in meeting the ordinary expenditure that it would be the height of folly to add another burden to already over-burdened shoulders."

But the Belfast Council of Social Welfare were troubled by the fact that the number of cases of hospital patients in which recovery was retarded because they received no aftercare was rapidly increasing. In many instances, the necessary nourishment could not be provided by patients or their relatives. In others the home conditions were such that the patient could not possibly progress, and was quickly becoming as ill as ever. The Council decided that something would have to be done, and that it must come through an agency outside the hospitals.

So a committee was formed of representatives nominated by each of the voluntary hospitals, the Belfast Council of Social Welfare, and societies connected with the relief of the sick.[23]

The first almoner employed by this Committee was unqualified, but in January 1938, an almoner who had trained under the auspices of the Association of Hospital Almoners in London was appointed. Later that same year the Royal Victoria Hospital in Belfast was also to appoint its first qualified almoner and she quickly set about developing the service and expanding her team during the war years. During this time the Hospitals' After-care Committee continued to employ an almoner and the liaison which had developed with hospitals in terms of support to patients needing help with special diets, or follow-up visits after discharge, proved invaluable at a time when many people were still leading a grossly deprived existence under the Poor Law system.

Indeed, until the establishment of the National Health Service in 1948, medical treatment was not free except in Poor Law Infirmaries. Many employed people subscribed a weekly sum through their employer which entitled them and the members of their families to free treatment. For others, however, treatment was paid for on an assessment basis and this assessment was carried out by almoners, although the latter tried to view the patients' needs as their real priority at all times.

During war-time the impact of the supportive almoner service continued to spread. In 1942 one of the staff employed in the Royal Victoria Hospital left to work at the Emergency Service Hospital which had been set up by the Government for the treatment of war casualties, including civilians injured in air-raids. This EMS Hospital was eventually transferred in 1945 from the grounds of Purdysburn Psychiatric Hospital to Musgrave Park Hospital, where there was also provision for patients suffering from tuberculosis and patients with orthopaedic conditions.

Another landmark for the service occurred in 1943 when the Belfast Hospital for Sick Children decided to start an Almoners' Department and appointed a qualified worker.

During this same year, the six almoners who were working in Belfast decided to form a group which would meet on a monthly basis in private houses or in the offices of the Belfast Hospitals' After-care Committee. It was recorded in the minutes of the first meeting that "this group joined together from mutual interest and also because they thought the opportunity to discuss the problems they met in their work would be useful and that their united opinion about various social difficulties would be likely to carry more weight than that of individual members." [24]

Miss M E Hall was elected as the first chairperson of the group which was shortly afterwards to receive the sanction of the Hospital Almoners' Association in London.

The Work of the Belfast Council of Social Welfare

As a result of the First World War, there had been a wave of idealism fostering a belief that organized effort could present the solutions to poverty and destitution. It was because of its wish to play its part on this new optimistic social order that the Belfast Charity Organization Society had changed its name to the Council of Social Welfare, reflecting its intention to widen its scope. In effect we have witnessed from the earlier Annual Report quotations how most of the time and energy of the Council was taken up in coping with the immense distress caused by the extensive unemployment in the 1920s. A survey conducted by the Council in 1929 estimated that in Belfast alone over 2,000 families were utterly destitute, depending on begging, charity hand-outs or the Board of Guardians' limited outdoor relief.

The newly constituted Distress Committee of the Council then pressurized the Board of Guardians, Belfast Corporation and the Government to take more urgent action. Through making their information public, they also raised substantial money for relief. Boots, clothing and blankets were collected and distributed and many farmers transported produce in from the countryside without any charge.

Other schemes which were initiated by the Council included the Belfast Hospitals' After-care Committee, which, as we have seen, had such an important contribution to make eventually to the development of the almoners' service. They also pioneered the provision of free legal advice and later actual legal representation for people who would otherwise have been unable to afford it — the so-called "Poor Man's Lawyer" service. An article in the *Northern Whig* on 6 May 1936 illustrated the wide range of activities being engaged upon by the council. "A report from the Executive Committee presented by the Chairman, Professor A Macbeath MA, showed that in addition to the normal work of the Council, (1) steps were being taken by the Council to establish a Poor Man's Lawyer Department, and that they were in communication with the Incorporated Law Society of Northern Ireland regarding the matter; (2) that they had made representation to the Ministry of Home Affairs regarding improvements in the law governing house-to-house collections and (3) that the Council had called a conference of social workers interested in children and young people, and had made recommendations to the Committee set up by the Home Office to review legislation dealing with Children and Young Offenders.

> "It was further reported that the Executive Committee had under consideration the desirability of an increase in the number of nursery schools, and the provision of facilities for training social workers in Belfast... In the discussion which followed, various social workers called attention to the social problem caused by the large number of young people who were unable to get employment for years after they had left school and urged that this problem should be taken into consideration by the Council." [25]

In an attempt to bring home the point forcibly to the public authorities about the lack of good quality working class houses, the Council used a donation of £20,000 to erect model houses which were then made available to families at a less than economic rent.

The positive and stimulating effect of the Belfast Council of Social Welfare is amply illustrated in one case example. In 1938, a shipyard worker contracted tuberculosis and needed to go to a sanatorium for several months. However his insurance benefit was not sufficient to maintain his wife and young children and the Council decided to make a weekly allowance to the family until he was restored to health. At the same time his workmates had on their own initiative collected some money to help the family. When they heard from his wife about the Council's involvement, they approached the Council to ask about the source of the funds. Having heard that the burden was entirely met through voluntary donations, the shipyard workers decided to assist the Council's work and their action influenced other firms to do the same. As a result the Council received as much as £1,000 per year from workers' contributions until the late 1940s.

Another pioneering venture initiated by the Council was the establishing of the first free Citizens Advice Bureau in Belfast in the 1940s. Bureaux had been set up all over Britain under the auspices of the National Council of Social Service at the outbreak of war because of the need for information centres to counter the disorganization of community life. The Council's initiative, acting as a local representative of the NCSS, was later to mushroom into a wide network of free advice services throughout the Province.

Concerned that there were no opportunities in the Province for "theoretical studies of social questions", the Council had by 1939 commenced a series of lectures on various aspects of social work, with invited speakers attending from various bodies such as the Unemployment Assistance Board and the Board of Guardians. It was in effect a rudimentary but pioneering staff development programme in social work practice. In addition the Council had opened its doors to "centres of social study" outside Northern Ireland who sent their students for practical training for anything from a month to a year. Indeed it was largely because of the Council's encouragement that Queen's University Belfast was to introduce a School of Social Studies to increase the number of trained social workers in the Province.

And behind the scenes there was continuous advocacy from the Council, whether in relation to juvenile court constitution, the need for more probation officers, or a more extensive home help service for mothers in poor health.[26]

The Formation of the Northern Ireland Council of Social Service

The Northern Ireland Council of Social Service was formed in 1938 with the expressed objectives of co-ordination and development of existing provincial and local social services; undertaking research; encouraging with financial or material help the formation of social service and community organizations. At the outset the Council was to have particular regard to problems arising from unemployment. In its first meeting the immediate task of the Council was seen to be to co-ordinate scattered effort in combatting the psychological effects of "prolonged idleness". It was established that £3,000 per year would be provided by the Government to supplement public subscriptions. However it was seen as an independent body outside the control of Government, although operating in conjunction with the Ministry of Labour.

Its main initiatives in relation to unemployment appear to have consisted of promoting "Welfare Clubs" and "Camps". Employing peripatetic instructors in carpentry and physical education, they sought to develop cultural and educational activities in these clubs which appeared to vary greatly in enthusiasm. The Council also committed itself to a camping programme having been influenced by the philosophy of the YMCA camps which had been operating for some years.

A report on the work of the YMCA camps is interesting in that it outlines principles which seem to have been adopted enthusiastically by the new NICSS.

> "It will be noted that the camps combine three features of importance in dealing with the psychological problems of unemployment: an opportunity to do useful work; contact with men from different social levels and from all parts of the Province; life in the open air with good food and regular exercise".[27]

By 1939, 1,407 men and boys were attending 26 camps, doing work such as land drainage, or preparing scenic beauty spots. A Central Allotments Committee was also set up to develop the interest of unemployed men in the cultivation of garden plots. There is a bland assumption underlying these activities that endeavours for "the good of the community" could help the unemployed to feel that they were discharging some useful function and that this would keep the stress of being unemployed at a manageable level. Psychological adaptation to the given circumstances was emphasized, rather than any analysis of the need for fundamental changes in the structures which caused and perpetuated poverty and unemployment.

(The NICSS carried on alongside the statutory personal social services after the Second World War, co-ordinating voluntary social service in relation to welfare of children, elderly, handicapped, and promoting the meals-on-wheels service.)

Immediately prior to the Second World War, there were many areas of life in which the people of Ulster compared very unfavourably with the United Kingdom.

Prevention and treatment of the health of the population presented a striking example. By 1939 there were 12 District Hospitals, 12 unconverted Union Infirmaries, 6 County Infirmaries and a few voluntary institutions. In the Union Infirmaries, the mortality rate was still high, and this reflected the continuing poor staffing and inadequate equipment. (In 1938 there were 2,317 deaths in poor law institutions which represented 13% of all deaths in Northern Ireland.) Tuberculosis caused 46% of all deaths in 1938 between the ages of 15-25 and 38% of those between 25-35. Only three of the Counties and County Boroughs provided sanatoria between the wars.

The Maternity Services was still a grossly neglected area because of lack of money and poor administration. In fact the maternal mortality rate in 1938 revealed that Northern Ireland had not only a higher rate than anywhere in the British Isles but there was a greater risk of death in childbirth in Ulster at this time than there was in 1921. The infant mortality rate remained second only to Scotland in the British Isles. The

The Inter-War Years

Maternity Service was still provided through the Poor Law and it is estimated that one in every four infants who died in Northern Ireland in the late 1930s were in the workhouses.

As estimate which emerged from the Ministry Inspectorate in the early 1940s was that there were nearly 10,000 mental defectives in Northern Ireland of whom 3,000 needed institutional care. But even by this stage there was no institution specifically to cater for their needs, nor any legal provisions especially to safeguard their interests and welfare as the Mental Treatment Act of 1932 did not specifically apply to the care of the mentally handicapped. In practice, most mentally defective children went to ordinary schools or stayed in their own homes. Those over school age who were not with relatives were to be found in workhouses, industrial schools, prisons and mental hospitals.

We have seen how in the field of mental health legislation some progress was made. However the inheritance in certain parts of the Province of antiquated accommodation was still posing problems.

In general health services remained mediocre by British standards and the combination of Ulster sectarian politics cutting across identification of urgent priorities and the vast fragmentation of administrative responsibility across the Ministries of Home Affairs, Labour, Education and Agriculture contributed in no small way to this.

The same reluctance to consider common interests across narrow religious and political lines was also seen in education. By the late 1930s there were no Education Committee Nursery Schools, poor medical services in schools, no special classes and a scanty number of scholarships available for secondary education. Most of the managers of the voluntary schools refused to transfer their schools or accept the Joint School Management Committees which were a prerequisite for grant assistance. Consequently more than half of the public elementary schools were voluntary and literally hundreds of schools were in as bad a plight in terms of accommodation and amenities as they were in 1920. (Underlying the reluctance to transfer was the intractable issue of religious education, and the usual associated mutual distrust between the Northern Irish).

Conclusion

As far as social welfare services were concerned, the picture as the Thirties came to a close was equally uninspiring from the point of view of governmental statutes and initiatives. Many pious hopes had been expressed but for reasons no doubt ranging from lack of finance to apathy and disinterest, few of these hopes had been realized. Many old, feeble-minded and children were still living and dying in workhouses in spite of strong pleas to abolish them and indeed the entire Poor Law system. The outmoded categories of industrial and reformatory schools still remained. Many children and old people still depended to a great extent for support and succour on the voluntary organizations in the form of subsistence to survive at home or residential care when homeless. The actual principal legislation relating to children echoed back to the beginning of the century in its content and philosophy. As for the probation service, its growth had remained stunted and it appeared to be subject to a strikingly unresponsive administration. However there were glimmers of recognition appearing in the Probation and Almoner Services of the need for a trained professional approach to social work, and Queen's University Belfast was to have an important vanguard role to play in this respect after the war. Meanwhile what flair and imagination did exist tended to be shown by voluntary groups. No doubt much of the work of such groups was motivated by a Christian crusading zeal, or reflected assumptions which justified being paternalistic to the deserving and eligible poor and judgemental towards the undeserving. Nonetheless it was largely due to such bodies as the Belfast Council of Social Welfare that both local and central government were reminded of their responsibilities towards their own relatively deprived and depressed community, and were constantly urged to take urgent rectifying action.

CHAPTER II
References

1 Oliver, J A (1978), *Working at Stormont*, Dublin Institute of Public Administration.
2 Lawrence, R J (1965), *The Government of Northern Ireland*, Clarendon Press Oxford.
3 Ibid.
4 Ibid.
5 *Annual Report 1924*, Belfast Council of Social Welfare.
6 *Annual Report 1927*, Belfast Council of Social Welfare.
7 Budge, J and O'Leary, C (1973).
Belfast-Approach to Crisis 1613-1970, McMullan.
8 *Progress in Ulster since 1921* Town and Country Development Committee Northern Ireland Council of Social Service.
9 *Report of the Departmental Commission on Local Government Administration*, 1927, Cmnd 73.
10 *Report on the Administration of Local Government Services*, 1928/29, Cmnd 110.
11 Ibid.
12 Paor, Liam de, (1969), *Divided Ulster*, Penguin.
13 *Annual Report 1929*, Belfast Council of Social Welfare.
14 Farrell, Michael, (1978), *The Poor Law and the Workhouse in Belfast 1834-1948*. Northern Ireland Public Records Office.
15 *Report of the Departmental Committee on the number and character of committals to Reformatory and Industrial Schools and provision of a Borstal 1923*, Cmnd 14.
16 *Adoption Bill, Second Reading*, 1929, Northern Ireland House of Commons.
17 *Children (Amendment) Bill*, Second Reading, Northern Ireland House of Commons.
18 *Report of the Committee on the Protection and Welfare of the Young and the Treatment of Young Offenders*, (1938), Cmnd 187.
19 Beresford, J O, (1976), *Some considerations on the Amalgamation or otherwise of the Northern Ireland Probation and After-care Service into the personal social services system in Northern Ireland*, unpublished thesis, NUU Coleraine, November.
20 *Mental Treatment Bill, Second Reading*, 1932, Northern Ireland House of Commons.
21 Ibid.
22 Ibid.
23 *Belfast Newsletter*, 26 November, 1936.
24 Much of the above material is based on a personal communication from Miss M. E. Hall.
25 *Northern Whig*, 6 May 1936.
26 MacBeath, A A, *Fifty Years of Social Work 1906-1956 — a brief history of the work of Belfast Council of Social Welfare*, Nicholson & Bass.
27 Newe, G B, (1963), *The story of the Northern Ireland Council of Social Service 1938-1963*, NICSS.

Chapter II – Appendix
Summary of Major Social Legislation

1920	Government of Ireland Act.
1920	Blind Persons Act (NI).
1924	Illegitimate Children Affiliation Orders Act (NI).
1925	Widows, Orphans and Old Age Contributory Pensions Act (NI).
1925	Old Age Pensions Act (NI).
1926	Malone Training School Act (NI).
1928	Legitimacy Act (NI).
1928	Poor Relief (Exceptional Distress) Act (NI).
1929	Adoption of Children Act (NI).
1931	Children (Amendment) Act (NI).
1932	Mental Treatment Act (NI).
1934	Exceptional Distress (Transitional Provisions) Act (NI).
1934	Adoption of Children (NI) (Workmens Compensation) Act (NI).
1935	Summary Jurisdiction and Criminal Justice Act (NI).
1937	Poor Relief (Amendment) Act (NI).
1938	Criminal Lunatics Act (NI).
1938	Blind Persons Act (NI).

Chapter III
Welfare and Bureaucracy

Social Work and the Welfare State

As we have seen, social work in Northern Ireland up to the Second World War existed in many forms and was not open to convenient definition. For instance the distinction between social work and religious movements was not always clear. Various religious groups had actively been contributing towards the personal welfare of individuals in keeping with their own assumptions and pastoral concern. There had also been no specific organizational context within which social work had its base, although there were similarities of aims and interests between different bodies. Thus the Belfast Council of Social Welfare, the Almoners' Service and the embryonic probation service shared a common purpose in terms of trying to improve standards of practice and achieve better and more extensive professional training, while they retained different traditions and objectives. These various strands of social work had developed as in the United Kingdom from the late nineteenth century onwards, trying to provide ways of alleviating human problems which were an alternative to the old traditional ideas of the philanthropic rich giving to the deserving poor. The road which social work in Northern Ireland was now to tread has to be seen in the historical context of overall developments in Great Britain. After the Second World War, the State was to be invested with powers over the individual citizen which had only been rivalled in the past during wartime. As P Seed puts it:

> "The State was entrusted to introduce and to sustain through the enactment and embodiment of welfare that universal harmony of social interest which philanthropists in the nineteenth century had vainly striven for through voluntary effort".[1]

The origin of the "Welfare State" – a term apparently coined by the Archbishop of Canterbury in 1941 – is significant in terms of social work's future role. In essence, it represented a Utopian ideal which everyone should strive for. It has been suggested that this ideal was the ultimate justification for the British going to war — to fight for the best of all possible worlds. The concept of the Welfare State related to both actual social welfare provision and the idea of the State itself as the provider of welfare — and the principal systems of provision were to include health, education, housing, social

A Service for People

security and welfare benefits. Attitudes to the expansion of social legislation, in Northern Ireland as in the rest of Britain, were diverse. On the one hand there was the view that social reform acted as a sort of antidote to socialism or even social revolution. J R Hay makes the point that employers had an interest in welfare as social benefits and the setting up of welfare institutions could also be a way of undermining militancy, coupled with attractive employee schemes in industry. [2] On the other hand, there had been growing pressure from organized labour and the Trades Union Congress had a definite influence on the setting up of the Beveridge Committee in 1941, which was to outline a plan for the creation of a comprehensive and unified system of social insurance. In addition, the Labour Government's social legislation from 1945–1948, the basis of the Welfare State, arose out of much war-time social planning, the Labour Party having played an active part in wartime Government. General attitudes ranged from welcome of change to entrenched principles which still echoed back to the Poor Law assumptions of the previous century.

The Northern Irish Parliament in keeping with its step-by-step relationship with Westminster set about introducing several Acts to build up and improve the Social Services, and thus implement its own version of the Welfare State. In this context, social work could either be regarded as a potentially redundant force or an important mediating influence for individual citizens. Mrs Irene Calvert MP for Queen's University Belfast and a member of the Northern Ireland Council of Social Service firmly took the second view in the Stormont House of Commons!

> "...History has decided that the doctor and the teacher have now become recognized persons of standing in the community, and the welfare officer who has to have very high educational qualifications and a period of training has unfortunately not received that recognition... I think the difficulty arises because most people do not understand the meaning of the word "welfare"... I think most people still imagine that the welfare officer is a very well-meaning busybody who goes around delivering hot soup to the deserving poor... Welfare work consists in providing the link between the family, the education service, the health service and the employment service... therefore it is necessary to know a great deal about legislation, about all the voluntary social service agencies that are working in a particular field." [3]

Mrs Calvert was clearly trying to define the role of the welfare officers who were starting to be employed by the new welfare authorities in terms of protecting the interests of the family and ensuring that they had knowledge of and were able to benefit from the range of statutory and voluntary services being made available. In the course of this chapter we shall investigate how this role was developed as welfare organizations became larger and more complex. The impact of the trend towards professional training will also be examined. Related to this, the difficulties encountered by professional social workers in the face of civil disturbances and the ethical and personal issues which have been brought to the fore will be discussed. Another major theme will be an analysis of the relationship between statutory Personal Social Services and the voluntary organizations which had either continued in existence after the war or which were to be formed at various stages with varying objectives in mind.

The Growth of Statutory Services in Northern Ireland

As we saw in the last chapter, welfare services had remained fairly static between the wars, mainly due to financial constraints. There were limited signs of the beginnings of professional social work with the development of a probation service and the appointment of a very small number of medical and psychiatric social workers. After the Second World War the Public Health and Local Government (Administrative Provisions) Act (Northern Ireland) 1946 created a new administrative structure to carry out the functions of the Boards of Guardians. County and County Borough Councils were required to provide welfare authorities acting through statutory welfare committees. Each area was to appoint a welfare officer and assumed responsibilities that had formerly rested with the Boards of Guardians. This re-structuring was made necessary by the postwar legislative 'explosion' referred to above which for the first time provided a comprehensive statutory framework within which mandatory duties and permissive powers were clearly defined. These Acts also made explicit the various groups with whom social work should be concerned: the elderly, the disabled, children, the mentally ill and the mentally handicapped.

At the risk of being labelled reductionist, one could divide the years 1950–1980 into four periods:

1   1950–1960:   The immediate problem the services were faced with was the dismantling of the Poor Law and workhouse system which had been in existence virtually unchanged for over a century. This necessarily involved an emphasis on establishing new institutions, old people's homes, children's homes, hostels and so on, possibly at the expense of staff development. The exception was on the hospital front, where medical and psychiatric social work became well established.

2   1960–1970:   This was a period of professionalisation in Local Authority social work and this professionalism calling into question the rationale of some

of the institutional services being provided (to give one example, large children's homes).

3   1970–1973: a brief but hectic period when the civil disturbances created a quite exceptional ferment, the positive aspects of which were not, unfortunately, capitalized on.

4   1973–1980: this period which, not altogether by design, brought the bureaucratisation of social work and the fairly unhappy marriage (or re-marriage) with health services.

A — BUILDING A NEW FOUNDATION

The most relevant pieces of immediate postwar legislation were the Welfare Services Act (Northern Ireland) 1949 and the Children and Young Persons Act (Northern Ireland) 1950.

The Welfare Services Acts

The terms of reference of the 1949 Welfare Services Act are described in the preamble to it:

> "An Act to substitute for the existing Poor Law, relating to workhouse accommodation and relief, provisions requiring welfare authorities to provide residential and other accommodation for certain persons in need thereof; to provide for the disposal of workhouse property, to make further provision for the welfare of handicapped, sick and aged persons..."

Consequently, the Act clearly identified the groups by whom welfare services might be required:

(a) persons who "by reason of age, infirmity or any other circumstance are in need of care and attention which are not otherwise available to them". This was a comprehensive brief and could include the elderly, the disabled, the mentally ill and the mentally subnormal;

(b) homeless persons (temporary accommodation);

(c) the disabled are defined more closely: blind, deaf or dumb, substantially and permanently handicapped by illness, injury or congenital deformity.

The services which could be made available were also spelt out:

(i) residential accommodation;

(ii) temporary accommodation;

(iii) in the case of disabled people:

    (a) to inform them of services,

    (b) for giving them in their own homes or elsewhere instruction in methods of overcoming the effects of their disabilities,

    (c) for providing workshops and hostels,

    (d) for providing them with suitable work in their own home or elsewhere,

    (e) to help them dispose of the produce of their work,

    (f) to provide recreational facilities,

    (g) to compile and maintain registers of disabled people;

(iv) to provide domestic help "for any person who being aged or handicapped lives either alone or in circumstances in which proper care and attention would but for such help not be available to them";

(v) Procedure was established for the compulsory removal of people who are in need of care and attention and also are a risk to themselves or others;

(vi) to protect the property of hospital patients and others in residential accommodation.

Interestingly enough, Section 20 of the Act imposed a duty on the welfare authority:

> "To ascertain from time to time the number of persons who ... are in need of services"

and

> "to disseminate information"

Mrs I Calvert MP, while accepting this Act as a necessary first step in the transition from the Poor Law, criticized it on the basis that it artificially categorized groups in need. She asserted that Northern Ireland had lost the opportunity to launch a properly integrated family service.[4]

This Act was fairly quickly extended by the Welfare Services Act (Northern Ireland) 1954 which in particular refined arrangements for domestic help. It included households containing "a person who is ill, an expectant mother, aged, mentally defective or a child of school age, a person who is blind, deaf or dumb or otherwise... handicapped."

The Act was still further extended by the Welfare Services (Amendment) Act (Northern Ireland) 1961 which added the provision of meals for the elderly and handicapped and the provision of recreational facilities for the elderly. There were also detailed regulations for the registration of private homes for the "aged, infirm or disabled".

The Way Ahead for Child Care

The publication of the Government White Paper "The Protection and Welfare of the Young and the treatment of the Young Offender" in 1946 constituted an important appraisal of the services for children and young persons.[5]

Hitherto the Boards of Guardians had come to assume the care of not only pauper children but orphan and deserted children. Statutory authority was vested in relieving officers to enable them to bring orphans or deserted children to the workhouses. The children were either maintained there by the Guardians or boarded-out with foster parents. Where parents were believed to be "unfit" and receiving relief in the workhouse, the Boards of Guardians also had the power to take over the control of the children. The principal act remained the 1908 Children Act. In addition, the Guardians' authority to board-out children was derived from the Pauper Children (Ireland) Acts of 1898 and 1902, which also enabled the payment of a cash allowance to the foster parents for the children's maintenance.

At this point, too, most of the residential homes for children were provided by voluntary religious organizations and the Government only had limited powers to intervene. Some changes were taking place: since 1942 the Juvenile Court structure was modified, in keeping with the spirit of the Lynn Report, to allow for two lay "children's guardians" to sit with the resident Magistrate in each Petty Sessions District. As for the Reformatory and Industrial Schools, the Ministry of Home Affairs remained responsible for certification and the Local Authorities were liable for the maintenance of children from their areas.

The 1946 White Paper makes the point that for well over a century there had been a reliance on voluntary effort and Poor Law facilities in caring for neglected and other children and that in a way knowledge of the extent of the problems had been kept in the background as a result. While referring to the importance of the Curtis Committee and Children Bill in England, the White Paper asserts that "the answer to the problem as it exists in Northern Ireland does not lie in a slavish adoption of the system, either existing or proposed, in Great Britain."[6] It was emphasized as a first essential that there should be one Government Department, the Ministry of Home Affairs, with responsibility for all legislation relating to children and young persons. An advisory committee known as the "Child Welfare Council" was to be appointed, to consider through time a variety of issues at the request of the Minister. It was also advised that welfare authorities should appoint sub-committees solely to deal with statutory duties in relation to children and young persons. Welfare authorities were urged to establish their own Children's Homes and the devising of realistic boarding-out payment rates to foster parents to be regularly reviewed by the Child Welfare Council was advocated.

It was in this White Paper that possibly the first post-war statement about the importance of education and training appeared:

> "In order that properly trained staff will be available to carry out the functions allocated to welfare authorities, the authorities will be empowered to arrange for the attendance of staff at suitable training courses."[7]

It was of course to take a considerably longer time before secondment on to full-time training courses was to be implemented in any substantial way. It was announced too that steps were being taken to consolidate regulations and statutes concerning adoption. Advertisements were to be prohibited which arranged or sought adoptions outside the authority of the adoption agencies which were now to be registered. It was also stated that voluntary homes were to be subject to formal registration and it was indicated that every attempt should be made to board-out children in foster homes. This policy stance was to be embodied in all children's legislation from that stage.

Other indications about future action included a re-appraisal of the age of criminal responsibility and an extension of the role of probation officers in Juvenile Courts. It was noted however that, outside Belfast, the probation service was still being operated by part-time officials and there was a recommendation that, while increased expenditure was to be made available to the probation service, the welfare authorities would be asked to assist with some of the work as an interim measure. As for the Reformatory and Industrial Schools, it was announced that these old distinctions were to be abolished and there was to be a system of approved schools classified for the various age groups. The two tables on page 74 indicate the number of children and young persons in various forms of care at this time.

The Children and Young Persons Act 1950

The White Paper paved the way for the Children and Young Persons Act (Northern Ireland) 1950 which was to bring Northern Ireland into closer line with England and Wales (at least in theory). The Children Act 1948 had led to the setting up of separate

TABLE 19 : Children under the care of the Welfare Authorities

	1939	1940	1941	1942	1943	1944	1945	1946
Workhouses	214	188	147	154	133	201	212	187
Boarded-out	364	349	372	339	328	315	293	312
Certified Schools	7	7	6	6	6	6	6	2
Total	585	544	52	499	467	522	511	501

TABLE 20 : Population of Reformatory and Industrial Schools

3lst December	Industrial Schools	Reformatories	Voluntary Schools
1938	271	107	234
1939	267	108	237
1940	267	134	225
1941	287	165	222
1942	323	181	229
1943	341	166	238
1944	340	155	243
1945	330	124	237
1946	294	112	221
1947	296	87	224

Local Authority Children's Departments in England and Wales. In contrast, the Northern Ireland Act was to be implemented by the 'generalist' welfare authorities under the guidance of the Ministry of Home Affairs. Having failed to introduce an equivalent Act to the 1933 Children and Young Persons Act (England and Wales) which had extended considerably the provisions for children in need of care and protection, the Northern Ireland legislators filled the gap in the 1950 Act.

In effect a 'double test' in care and protection proceedings was introduced. This meant that as well as establishing that a child was "falling into bad associations" or "exposed to moral danger" or "beyond control", it was necessary in addition to prove that he had either no parents or parents who were "unfit" to exercise care or not "exercising proper care". A child was also deemed in need of care and protection if he had been or was likely to be the victim of an offence noted in the Act. These offences included neglect and bodily injury but a source of difficulty in practice was that it had to be proved that such actions were deliberate. As Eileen Evason puts it "the assumption embodied in these provisions was not that the interest of the child was the most important consideration but that the parents could not be deprived of their rights unless found guilty in some sense." [8]

In addition to spelling out the conditions defining children in need of care and protection, the Act outlined various alternatives open to a court to try to meet the child's best interests. These included committal to a fit person, which could be a Welfare Authority, or the making of a Supervision Order to be implemented by a probation officer. In keeping with the provisions of the 1948 Children Act, this Act also outlined the duty of the Welfare Authority to receive children under 17 years of age into care where they had no parent or guardian, or were abandoned or lost; or where their parents were "for the time being or permanently, prevented by reason of mental or bodily disease or infirmity or other incapacity or any other circumstances from providing for his proper accommodation, maintenance and upbringing – having established that the invervention of the welfare authority was necessary in the interests of the welfare of the child". (Section 81)

Section 90 gave a definite directive to welfare authorities that residential care was only to be provided for children where "it is not practicable or desirable for the time being to make arrangements for boarding-out". This commitment in favour of fostering as the best form of substitute care very much reflected the 1946 Curtis Committee recommendations in England and the clear guidelines given in the 1948 Children Act. It stems from reactions against the institutionalisation of children that had been a feature of the Poor Law systems and the prevailing research of such as Dr John Bowlby who had emphasized the dangers of maternal deprivation in young children without adequate substitute care.

This issue has been the subject of a continuous debate among professional social workers ever since, especially in the light of further research highlighting the extremely high 'breakdown' rate of fostering placements.

Another significant feature of the 1950 Act was the confirmation that welfare authorities were to appoint their own children's officers to carry out the functions of the Act.

The Act also reviewed the constitution and procedures in juvenile courts. It established that a Juvenile Court should sit either in a different building or room from other courts or on different days and at different times. With regard to the age of criminal responsibility, the Act put into effect the recommendation that this should be raised to eight years from seven years. As predicted, the Act also signalled the final abolition of the categories of Reformatory and Industrial Schools and Section 109 announced that "the Ministry may classify training schools according to the age of the persons for whom they are intended, the religious persuasion of such persons, the character of the education and training given therein, their geographical position, or otherwise as it thinks best calculated to secure that a person sent to a training school is sent to a school appropriate to his needs". There was a clear duty laid on Local Authorities individually or collectively, to make good any deficiencies in training school accommodation and facilities.

Accompanying the Act were several statutory Rules and Orders which in combination meant that at last Mooney's Compendium of the Poor Law in Ireland could be set aside in relation to the care of children and young persons.

(a) Boarding-out (No 43) 1950. As well as defining the procedures required in approving and maintaining contact with foster homes, these regulations also required the welfare authorities to report to the Ministry of Home Affairs if children had not been boarded-out within three months of admission, and apply for its consent to alternative arrangements. In other words, the Regulations pre-empted any professional decisions about the welfare of the child.

(b) Juvenile Courts (No 27) 1950. These Regulations spelt out requirements for the constitution of Juvenile Courts, and selection of panel members.

(c) Children's Officer (No 130) 1950. The required qualifications for such appointments were listed.

(d) Voluntary Homes (No 38) 1950. The particulars were outlined which had to accompany any application to the Ministry for the registration of a voluntary home under Part VI of the Act.

(e) Training Schools (No 57) 1950. A form was prescribed for the record of information in the possession of the court to be transmitted to the training school when a Training School Order was made.

(f) Welfare Authorities' Homes (No 130) 1952. Heralding the growth of the various welfare authority Children's Homes, these Regulations included requirements for visiting by the Welfare Committee and Children's Officer, duties of the medical officer and restrictions on the recording of corporal punishment, e. g. Section 12(3)(a)

"It shall be inflicted only on the hands or posterior with a light cane and shall not exceed six strokes in the case of a child over ten years of age, and two strokes in the case of a child over eight and under ten years of age."

(g) Voluntary Homes (No131) 1952. Similar requirements were imposed on the running of Voluntary Children's Homes. The Ministry of Home Affairs was also given the authority to limit the number of children who could at any one time be accommodated in a Home.

(h) Training Schools Rules (No 132) 1952. These Rules outlined the composition and duties of the Board of Management, staff duties and ongoing care and education needs of the residents. The Board of Management was also charged with ensuring that a suitable person should be appointed for each pupil "to carry out his or her after-care" when placed out on licence.

A New Adoption Act

As in the inter-war period, there does not appear to have been significant public pressure to bring adoption legislation in Northern Ireland more up to date although the Horsburgh Committee of 1939 had led to various legislative changes to tighten up procedures in England and Wales. Nonetheless in 1950 the Adoption of Children Act (Northern Ireland) was introduced by the Government. In keeping with the 1946 White Paper proposals, the new Act prohibited the making of arrangements for adoption by any "body of persons" other than a welfare authority or a registered adoption society. (This did not prevent an individual from making arrangements). Apart from the general publicity of welfare authorities or adoption societies, advertisements were banned which indicated either that a person wished to adopt a child or that certain children were available to be adopted. Eileen Evason makes the point that while this Act was very similar to that enacted in England and Wales, there remained some significant differences.[9] For instance applicants had to be resident or domiciled in Northern Ireland whereas there was more flexibility in the English Act. Another distinguishing feature was that in Northern Ireland there were two Court Hearings. An Interim Order was made at the first and following a probationary period of not less than three months a Final Order could be made. This contrasted with the English system whereby, if the child had been in the care and possession of the applicant for at least three months beyond the age of six weeks old, an Adoption Order could be made at a single hearing.

This Adoption of Children Act was to remain in force for a further seventeen years. Accompanying it came further statutory rules and orders governing the procedures of the courts making Adoption Orders and the adoption societies applying for registration.

The Role of the Child Welfare Council

Under the 1950 Children and Young Persons Act, a Child Welfare Council was to be established with the duty of:

A Service for People

(a) advising the Ministry upon any matter referred to them by the Ministry in connection with the performance by the Ministry of its functions under this Act or under the Adoption of Children Act (Northern Ireland) 1950;

(b) making representations to the Ministry with respect to any matter affecting the welfare of children and young persons.

The various reports published by the Child Welfare Council proved to be important indicators of the currently prevailing situation in relation to services for children and young persons, although the qualitative content of the reports varied widely. The first report appeared in 1954 in the form of an "Interim Report" on "Juvenile Deliquency".[10] There is a certain inescapable irony when the Council states that: "Because of the mainly rural character of our community and its escape from some of the major disturbances of the war, juvenile crimes associated with violence are rarer here than in other parts of the United Kingdom." At the same time it was felt that the incidence of "juvenile delinquency" was serious enough to cause some concern. It was pointed out that the combined indictable and non-indictable offences among juveniles (including malicious damage, stealing, railway offences) had risen from 825 in 1938 to 1154 in 1953, an increase of 39.9%. However it was suggested that this increase could partly be accounted for by the fact that the 1950 Children and Young Persons Act had raised the upper age of young persons from 16 to 17 years.

A peculiar vacillation between needs for structural change and needs for spiritual uplift are apparent when the Council tries to identify causes for juvenile delinquency.

"It is (therefore) probable that poverty by itself is not a primary factor, but may be a powerful contributory factor in aggravating the bad home circumstances."

"Nothing has been done at home to give the child the peace and security of an ever–present faith." "... too often children are not taught by their parents to seek for help and guidance in their religion."

The Council went on to recommend that the Family Casework Service needed to be extended and urged the establishment of residential training houses "such as the Mayflower in Portsmouth". (The Salvation Army was in fact to open such a training home for families also called the Mayflower in Belfast). It also called for a Youth Advisory Service and the provison of community centres, adding a cautionary note that cinema and reading habits needed more control exercised over them! This report takes a pronounced moralistic and consensual stance in relation to the problems of the young. Environmental factors are highlighted but there is a strong emphasis on the feckless and pathological nature of some families and their responsibility in causing delinquency.

page 78

A further Report by the Child Welfare Council in 1956 on "Children in Care" gives some indication of the issues current at the time, although again the discussion is highly coloured by the members' particular views on the structure of society.[11] It was reported that in 1955 there were 2142 children in the care of welfare authorities, 963 of whom were boarded-out in foster homes. Amongst the children in residential children's homes it was felt that there must be a very large number of children who could have the "happiness and security of a normal family life" if suitable substitute parents could be found. The economic argument for boarding-out as a cheaper alternative also did not escape the Council's attention. A basic assumption behind the Council's recommendations was that "the child in care has a right to a house of his own as much like other children's as possible. Legal adoption is admittedly the best way of providing this, but where it is not possible, boarding-out is considered to be the best alternative". This sort of emphasis closely reflects the thinking in English Children's Departments at the time, where, as a matter of policy, the boarding–out of children in some instances led to closure of children's homes. The Council also emphasized that all possible safeguards should be taken to prevent abuse of children.

"Where an older child is placed in a foster house to which a farm or a business is attached, careful supervision is particularly important as a safeguard against possible exploitation."

At this stage, there were still many children being cared for by the voluntary organizations on a private basis and the Council called for greater co-ordination between these organizations and the welfare authorities. There was also an encouragement that welfare authorities should be prepared to take appropriate children in voluntary homes into care with a view to finding suitable foster houses for them.

Some of the final recommendations of this Council Report highlight the strong religious stencil which has tended to be stamped over discussions on social issues in Northern Ireland. It was suggested that it was important to allocate children to children's homes in line with their religious backgrounds. In addition, it was urged that welfare authorities "should take special steps to ensure that children in Welfare Authority Homes are provided with adequate and appropriate religious training by the appointment of a sufficient number of qualified persons on the supervision staff from both of the main religious communities in Northern Ireland". While the question of religious upbringing was also embodied in other British legislation, the former quotation reflects the head-counting preoccupation so peculiar to Northern Ireland.

A Framework for Mental Health Services

Just as the Welfare Services Act provided a comprehensive framework for services for the elderly and physically handicapped, the Mental Health Act (Northern Ireland) 1948 attempted to do the same for the mentally disordered. The Act distinguished between the mentally ill and the mentally subnormal. The emphasis for the former is on "prevention, diagnosis and treatment", while for the latter it was on "ascertainment, care, supervision, training and occupation".

The onus was on the newly constituted Hospitals' Authority to develop services and although reference is made to "settlement or resettlement in the community" the Hospitals' Authority inevitably showed a preference for institutional care.

Nevertheless the Act was progressive in seeking to make the availability of treatment more flexible. Three groups of patients were still distinguished: the certified (those who could be detained in hospital long-term); the temporary (those who could be detained against their will for a specified period of time, in the hope that treatment might be effective) and the voluntary. Attempts were made to reduce the number of certified patients and to extend the treatment period for temporary patients as a move to trying to ensure that they did not become 'certified'.

In spite of these progressive attitudes, the statutory Rules and Orders accompanying the 1948 Act make it clear that sometimes treatment methods were still primitive:

> "It shall not be lawful to use for the purposes of mechanical restraint any instrument or appliances other than the following:
>
> (a) a jacket or dress, laced or buttoned down the back, made of strong linen, having long outside sleeves fastened to the dress at the shoulders only; such sleeves having closed ends to which tapes may be attached for tying behind the patient's back when the arms have been folded across the chest;
>
> (b) gloves without fingers made of strong linen or chamois leather, padded or otherwise and fastened at the wrists with buttons or locks;
>
> (c) sheets or towels, when tied or otherwise fastened to the bed or other object."

Patients' rights were protected by a judicial procedure so that a welfare officer wishing to 'petition' for temporary treatment for a patient had to apply to a Resident Magistrate (or Justice of the Peace) for authority.

An effort was also made to remove stigmatizing terminology, such as 'lunatics, imbeciles' and so on; 'person requiring special care' was substituted for 'mental defective' and 'mental patient' for 'lunatic'.

Problems and Achievements in the New Welfare Departments

Implementation of all this new legislation presented the new welfare departments with mammoth problems. The late Miss Kay Forrest, who was to become the first welfare officer for Belfast in 1948, recalled the first impression of stunned shock which she experienced on being escorted around the workhouse within the Belfast City Hospital. She was greeted with the sight of so many children all sitting in rows, abnormally quiet and passive, with books held in front of them. She observed that many of the books were in fact upside down and it transpired that many of the children could not read. The children were still under the same roof as many other residents, including groups of elderly "mentally defective" and "pauper lunatics". Some of the female residents in fact helped to care for the children and it would appear that some of the employees were not exactly tuned in to the emotional needs of their charges. Miss Forrest acted on the premise that priority should be given to toddlers of 2–5 years of age in the workhouse as they suffered most from the dire lack of stimulation. Thus, with the relieving officers, several of whom joined the welfare authorities, she encouraged the expansion of boarding-out and the establishment of welfare authority residential homes more suited to children's needs.

Alongside the welfare authorities, the voluntary homes had been fulfilling a vital service in taking children on a private basis. Clearly the homes which originated through religious organizations had a strong sense of responsibility for the spiritual upbringing of the children. The differing emphasis in the objectives of such homes and those of the welfare authority were to result in a great deal of suspicion on both sides and it could be said that the ironing out of differences is a process which is still going on today.

The whole process of improving standards of care appears to have been very slow and gradual. Mr Tom Shannon recalled how, when he became the Superintendent of the Belfast Workhouse, re-named the Welfare Hostel in 1954, workhouses were still operating in Ballymena and Armagh. In his own establishment there were still over 300 "inmates" including illegitimate and orphaned children, unmarried mothers, prostitutes, mentally handicapped and elderly. The children were categorized as "accompanied" and "unaccompanied" (ie paupers, waifs and strays). It was indeed one of Mr Shannon's functions along with the matron-in-charge of the children to select suitable names for the abandoned infants. It is clear from Mr Shannon's account of the early stages in his post that he had formidable obstacles to overcome both in getting practical resources to improve the surroundings and in moving forward beyond stigmatizing attitudes. During his first tours of inspection "inmates" were still following the tradition laid down by previous "workhouse masters" and automatically stood to attention in his presence. There was also a fixed arrangement with the local police that he would take in "drunks" at night and release them in the morning, thus saving the police from having to make formal charges and attend court appearances.

A Service for People

Mr Shannon makes the point forcibly, however, that the people trying to implement welfare services at this stage had an enthusiastic commitment and clear visions of their objectives, even though their resources were scant and the amount of problems confronting them often overwhelming. He also pointed to the important background support which was still being given to the welfare authorities by voluntary groups. For instance, the North Belfast Mission, for all its religious motivation, was continuing through the leadership of the energetic Reverend Scott to provide relief to families and opened various residential and holiday homes. The Salvation Army too was continuing its dedicated tradition of caring for the homeless.[12]

Welfare departments are sometimes unfairly criticized for emphasizing institutional provision at the outset. This is not factually accurate as we shall see in discussing the home help service. But even if it were, it leaves out of account several important factors which helped to shape policy.

The first of these has already been mentioned: the absolute dearth of personnel. Here are two first-hand accounts of what it was like to work in Belfast's welfare department at its inception and in the early stages.

"On 11 March 1948, John Ewing and I were appointed as Children Act Inspectors by the newly-formed Belfast Corporation Welfare Committee.

We started off by dealing mainly with children nursed and maintained all over the City. Roughly, John did the boys and I did the girls. We had only public transport and at first, used our own money and were recouped. Morning tea was served in a room in the basement somewhere below the Town Clerk's Department and thence we adjourned at 10.30 if still in the "Hall".

The staff at the very outset consisted of the welfare officer, Miss K B Forrest – now Children's Inspector with the Ministry of Home Affairs, Mr Hall, doing blind welfare, Albert Holland, officially a clerical officer but really a general mine of information and Interviewer – when in difficulty we referred to Albert and he in turn referred to the Act – and ourselves. We were joined very soon by "Box and Cox" – Mr Coates and Mr Neill, who were specially designated to work with the aged and handicapped.

All the above, plus two senior administrative officers who acted as clerks to various corporation committees were accommodated in one small room (53) in the Town Clerk's Department in the City Hall, a small corner of which was boxed off and that – for the information of all who complain about inadequate interviewing space –was where we interviewed our clients. A lot of inquiries at first came from folk who thought we could help with housing problems. These we mostly re–directed to the Estates Department upstairs.

The Nursed and Maintained Register was a large black bound volume which contained the names of all the children at nurse in Belfast and which had certainly

Welfare and Bureaucracy

not been kept up to date. We waded through as best we could. We were not the investigating authority for the Adoption Court in those days but we did board-out and a monthly report on all boarded-out children in the City had to be submitted to committee. Being a small staff we knew about each other's difficult cases and it was natural that at times we got involved in other things – for instance John Ewing and I used to go one morning per week to the Welfare Hostel, Lisburn Road, to hand over the pocket money to the residents.

In 1950 we moved from our cramped quarters to what appeared to us spacious accommodation in nissen huts at 80a May Street." [13]

"In 1953 we moved from our nissen hut to 133 Royal Avenue, a few doors from the Corporation's Lost Property Office whence clients who had lost their way were constantly being redirected to us.

My own memories of those days in Royal Avenue are a confused blur of toiling up rickety stairs to the third (or was it the fifth?) floor; of polite bickerings among the Welfare Visitors over the boundary lines of their work (there were three Welfare Visitors but one was later promoted to the job of Boarding-out Officer, leaving only two to cover the entire City, and the new Adoption Act to be implemented); of agonized appeals on my part for more field staff; or telephones endlessly ringing with requests to accommodate children ("you have a Nursery now; why can't you take Baby So-and-So? Her mother is a poor sort of creature and just doesn't know how to put on nappies properly"). Brefne Nursery at this time consisted only of No 49 and only took children between two and five years, the babies being accommodated in the old Welfare Hostel in wicker cots with rockers – hence the difficulty in receiving them into care, even when occasion warranted.

Older children were also accommodated in the Welfare Hostel which was beginning to burst at the seams so in 1957 the Committee bought a rather dilapidated mansion on the Antrim Road and moved 12 boys and two female attendants into it. Surprisingly it worked quite well for a time and at least gave the boys some kind of home life, although a sharp eye was kept on the budget. I can remember once receiving a curt inquiry from someone (in the City Hall, I suppose) asking was it really necessary for the boys to have currant buns for tea? I don't remember what my official reply was but I do remember my unofficial reaction.

When the time came for us to move into College Street, we were already quite a sizeable Department, large enough to fill the third floor of No 16 to capacity. I had got another Welfare Visitor and a new Children's Home for school–age boys and girls about to be opened as well as the babies' extension in Brefne."[14]

Secondly, there were the attitudes of Councillors on Welfare Committees. These could be moralistic and it is reasonable to suppose that the most 'visible' groups should be considered first. These obviously included the elderly, the blind, the children

A Service for People

at risk. For other groups, Poor Law attitudes died hard. These included the homeless, 'problem families', the mentally ill, and homeless single persons.

Thirdly, the new Departments were set very firmly in the context of Local Government, and committees very properly had a strong sense of responsibility to the ratepayer. All expenditure had therefore to be gradual and justified.

The top priority was seen as accommodating elsewhere the inhabitants of the workhouse, and two groups who had needed immediate attention were obviously the elderly and children.

The first developments in old people's homes used large mansion-type houses, usually set in their own grounds. These had the advantage of retaining something of the atmosphere of one's own home (as distinct from purpose-built homes). There were disadvantages: dormitory-type bedrooms; the difficulty of heating large communal rooms and, in particular, the shortage of ground floor bedroom accommodation. (The last named became an increasingly pressing problem.)

Because of the pressure to house quite a large number of elderly people, the tendency was to plan for large homes. For example, Abbeydene, on the Shore Road, Belfast was originally scheduled to accommodate 84 residents while the first purpose-built home (Ben Madigan) opened with 92 places.

There were significant changes in thinking over this ten-year period:

(a) towards smaller units,
(b) towards purpose-built homes,
(c) towards building homes as an integral part of the community.

Domiciliary services were by no means neglected. The memorandum accompanying the 1949 Welfare Services Act clearly stated the importance of keeping elderly and disabled people in their own homes.

The history of the home help service possibly hindered early developments. In its origins it was essentially a professional, almost paramedical service. There were two groups of paid domestic help – commonly known as "mother and baby" home helps and "TB" home helps. The first were to help with home confinements and to help mothers with newly born babies. The "TB" home helps were a panel of specially selected and screened home helps who gave assistance in households where there was a person with tuberculosis.

Understandably enough at this time the domestic help service was provided by the Health Department. Consequently the newly established Welfare Committee rather brushed it to one side. "In view of the fact that the Health Authority already operates a Home Help Scheme it has been suggested... that they should extend the existing

page 84

scheme to include aged persons and others in need of care and attention who come within the scope of Section 43 of the Health Services Act. This they have agreed to do."

The amended Welfare Services Act of 1954 placed the responsibility for the home help service squarely with Welfare Committees. Coinciding with the control of tuberculosis, this led to a decline in the use of the service as a 'medical' aid and its considerable expansion as a social service, mainly with the elderly. At the 'handing over' date of September 1954, only households with

(a) children under five,
(b) elderly and handicapped people living alone and in receipt of State Benefits,
(c) persons suffering from tuberculosis could be provided with home help.

The new arrangements meant that the Service could become more flexible. Home helps themselves were employed as "full-time", "part-time", or "casual". The concept of the 'casual' home help (working two to four hours a day) was very much in keeping with the Ministry's original plans for a 'Good Neighbour' scheme helping elderly and disabled people to live in their own homes for as long as possible.

TABLE 21 : Persons accommodated in welfare department Old People's Homes in December of the year shown:

1951	1952	1953	1954	1955	1956	1957	1958	1959	1960	1962
238	418	601	695	764	789	886	957	1143	1185	1383[15]

However, domiciliary services were by no means neglected as the growth in the home help service in Table 22 clearly shows:

TABLE 22 : Number of households provided with homehelp in the year shown:

1950	1951	1952	1953	1954	1955	1956	1957	1958	1959	1960
298	520	741	1068	3000	4443	5047	5484	5613	6262	7057

1961	1962	1963
8281	9796	10518[15]

Services for the handicapped remained patchy and the number of persons registered as handicapped were fairly static until the early 1960s.

A Service for People

TABLE 23 : Number of persons registered handicapped in December of the year shown :

1950	1951	1952	1953	1954	1955	1956	1957	1958	1959	1960
4062	4646	4776	4850	4822	4661	4567	4812	4918	5188	5211

1961	1963
6072	8366[15]

Services for the disabled from 1950 onwards were patchy. Certain groups, notably the blind, were reasonably well catered for. Others, such as the deaf, had good services from voluntary organizations. Still others, commonly referred to as the "generally handicapped" (ie not blind, partially sighted, deaf, dumb or hard of hearing), were scarcely catered for at all.

There were historical reasons for this too. The Blind Persons Acts of 1920 and 1938 meant that a register of blind people had already been maintained and in 1950 there were some 950 people in Belfast on it. Two hundred and fifty of these were over 70 years of age. Quite extensive services were being provided:

(a) in conjunction with the Workshops for the Industrious Blind and the Ministry of Labour, blind people were trained and employed;

(b) there was also a Home Worker's Scheme;

(c) home instruction was given in braille (or moon) and handicrafts;

(d) grants were provided for residential care in the Home for the Blind and St Brigid's Home, Whiteabbey;

(e) free bus and train passes were available;

(f) in co-operation with the Wireless for the Blind, wireless sets were provided and licences paid for.

It is clear that, partly because of this earlier legislation, the blind were easily identifiable as a group which might be in need of services.

During the 1950s considerable progress was made therefore in providing a basic service both on the institutional front (old people's homes and children's homes) and in domiciliary services. For example, a useful measuring-rod of the state of child care services was a further Child Welfare Council Report of 1960 entitled "The Operation of the Social Services in relation to Child Welfare".[16]

It was noted that many children who had been abandoned or had no parent or guardian were survivors of the Poor Law era and the welfare authorities had assumed responsibility for their care.

Welfare and Bureaucracy

A survey of children in care was carried out by the Council for the period 1959-60 and the findings were contrasted with the situation in 1947, before the welfare committees had come into being.

Statistical Year –1947

- 1000 Children in the care of voluntary organizations (practically all of whom were in institutions)
- 501 Children in the care of Local Authorities (of whom 312 were boarded-out and 189 in workhouses or other institutions).

Statistical Year – 1959(60)

- 751 Total number of children in the care of voluntary organizations
- 1148 Total number of children in the care of welfare authorities

Of the 1148 children in welfare authority care there were:

- 724 boarded-out
- 226 in welfare authority homes
- 158 maintained in voluntary homes on behalf of welfare authorities.

It was felt that the figures of 1947 reflected the limited interpretation of responsibilities and priorities that were given to the care of children and the nature of the legislation that was being implemented by the Boards of Guardians.

From the 1959 figures it can clearly be seen that there was a substantial assumption of care by welfare authorities, provision of numerous residential establishments and a commitment to boarding-out of children. Belfast City had the lowest boarding-out rate of 43.9% and the Council concluded that "in centres of densest population such as Belfast the greatest difficulty is that suitable foster homes are less readily available". On the other hand it was noted that children in voluntary homes, apart from those in Dr Barnardo's care, were rarely boarded-out.

Discussing the role of voluntary homes in general, this Report concluded that the numbers of children in their care would continue to fall although they would probably have an important role to play in long-term cases where special treatment was needed or boarding out was not appropriate.

Some of the conclusions about available statistical data are of interest. The total number of children in care (2.4 per 1000) was lower than in England and Wales (5.2

per 1000) and Scotland (6.5 per 1000). The biggest single presenting reason for reception into care was illegitimacy. It was felt that the home help service was helping to keep down the numbers of short-term admissions to care. Once again it was emphasized that no children should remain in institutional care if substitute parents might be made available. The uneven development of child care facilities in the Province was reflected in the statement that thought needed to be given to the "divergences in the pattern of child care from one welfare authority to another; and as between welfare authorities and voluntary homes". There was also a call for the establishment of a central register at the Ministry of Home Affairs to record information about children in statutory and voluntary care. (This was to be implemented by way of annual returns to the Ministry of Home Affairs until the re-organization of services in 1973.)

In summary, the main features in the development of child care services during the first decade of statutory social services included: the dismantling of the Poor Law heritage, in terms of legislation, physical structure and attitudes, and the planned growth, albeit patchy and uneven, of welfare authority facilities; the preoccupation with boarding out of children as a policy in the best interests of children and the view that residential child care should be regarded at best as a short-term or temporary measure, unless there were special circumstances; the growing assumption of responsibility for the care of the children by welfare authorities leading to a reduction in the contribution of voluntary organizations; the beginning of a recognition that staff in personal caring roles in relation to children needed some form of training and preparation for their jobs.

Alongside the development of welfare authority services, social work in the medical and psychiatric settings and in the probation service was continuing to progress – and it is to these settings that we now turn our attention.

Almoners Established as Medical Social Workers

In 1943 the almoners working in the Belfast area began to have regular monthly meetings using the office accommodation of the Belfast Hospitals After-Care Committee. Although informal, an executive committee was formed and the group organized its own form of staff development programme with invited speakers addressing their seminars. In 1944 links were established with almoner colleagues working in Dublin and this led to joint meetings. At this time too discussions had been taking place in London for the formation of an Institute of Hospital Almoners' Association and this occurred in 1946.

Subsequently the almoners of Belfast and Dublin were to unite to form the Irish region of the new Institute which, as well as being a professional body had its own training school. Quarterly meetings were held in Dublin and relationships were notably friendly and co–operative. By the end of the Second World War the almoner tradition had already been established in the Royal Victoria Hospital and the Royal Belfast Hospital for Sick Children. In 1947 the almoner from the Royal Belfast Hospital for Sick Children went on to pioneer a new almoners' Department in Belfast City Hospital.

By 1948, the growth in the number of almoners in Belfast and the inception of the post-war Health and Social Services legislation led to the separation of the two Irish regions and the setting up of the Northern Ireland Regional Committee. Training was given an important priority and staff development was enhanced through the staging of conferences, and contributions to the "Almoner Journal". It is of interest to note that the Institute of Almoners in the early days required the Regional Committee to have a proportion of "lay" members and usually the Chairman was an eminent doctor. In effect the lay representation covered many professions but the medical profession appears to have provided the committee "life-blood". The Regional Committee had regular consultative liaison with the Northern Ireland Hospitals' Authority who in turn consulted them on various professional issues.[17]

Thus, as the Almoners' Service moved into the 1960s, various significant features had emerged. Arising from the early initiatives of the Belfast Hospitals' After-Care Committee, a network of almoners developed who placed strong emphasis on training and professional identity as a group. In keeping with earlier British pioneers of the almoner service they identified very closely with the medical profession, with its established code, language and estimable position. It is no coincidence that the first formal statements about the practice of social casework referred to "Study, Diagnosis and Treatment".

It would appear that, in accordance with earlier developments in Britain and America, it was social workers in the hospital setting who first began to define their professional roles and train to acquire their skills in any organized and lucid way in Northern Ireland. In 1964 the decision was taken to change the name "almoner" to "medical social worker" as a conscious attempt to identify more closely with the wider developing profession of social work.

Probation becomes a Full-time Service

As regards the probation service, the start of a full-time service in Northern Ireland was really heralded by the Probation Act (Northern Ireland) 1950. This gave the Ministry of Home Affairs full responsibility for the appointment of probation officers. Further structure was given to the service procedures in the form of Statutory Rules and Orders 1950 (No 58), which were cited as Probation Rules and gave guidelines on such matters as the content of Probation and Discharge forms. It has been suggested that the image of probation as a part-time voluntary exercise in Northern Ireland was a difficult one to cast aside and was revealed in a certain reluctance in Ministry circles to carry out rapid changes. Unlike England, Wales and Scotland, which had a local administration of the probation service, there was still a centralized administration of the Service in Northern Ireland through the Ministry of Home Affairs. (The recommendations of the earlier Lynn Committee for a Central Advisory Council and Probation Committees were not implemented.) It also seems possible that there were long-standing cultural attitudes in Northern Ireland which favoured retribution and incarceration for offenders and that these contributed to the retarded development of the service.

The 1950 Probation Act (Northern Ireland) replaced the Probation of Offenders Act of 1907. This Act detailed the grounds for and duration of probation orders and the various powers of the Court in relation to breaches of the Order. It was also established that where a person was in need of care or treatment within the spirit of the Mental Health Act (Northern Ireland) 1948, the Court could make a Probation Order which required treatment for a mental condition. The Ministry entered into a commitment to recruit and arrange for the training of further probation officers.

The under-developed nature of the service at this time is revealed in the fact that in 1948 there were 8 full-time and 4 part-time officers in post. Following the recommendations of the 1948 White Paper, County welfare officers started to act temporarily as probation officers. (This practice continued outside Belfast and Londonderry for the completion of social enquiry reports on juveniles.)

As indicated in Table 24, further caseload and staff establishment figures indicate that the change in the next decade was to be very gradual.

Thus the average caseload per officer was nearly 100 excluding social enquiry reports and matrimonial work, as compared with the recommendation of the Lynn Committee that officers should be carrying no more than 50–60 cases each "at the very most".

It is interesting to consider, alongside the slow progress of the probation service, the conclusions of the Child Welfare Council Report of 1960 on the "Operation of the Juvenile Courts in Northern Ireland".[19] Following the Children (Juvenile Courts) Act (Northern Ireland) 1942 which adopted the Lynn Report recommendation by allowing for the appointment of two lay "children's guardians" to sit alongside the resident magistrate, and the Children and Young Persons Act (Northern Ireland) 1950 which

page 90

TABLE 24 : Probation caseloads 1955–65.

Year	Caseloads		Staffing
1955	1279	persons on probation	14 full–time officers
	32	other supervision	1 part–time officer
	8	prison aftercare	
	4	Borstal aftercare	
1960	1843	persons on probation	19 full–time officers
	68	other supervision	1 part–time officer
	53	prison aftercare	
	4	Borstal aftercare	
1965	1980	persons on probation	20 full–time officers[18]
	82	prison aftercare	
	51	Borstal aftercare	
	1550	matrimonial cases	
	1344	social enquiry reports	

had looked at the overhaul of the Juvenile Courts, the Child Welfare Council was undertaking a timely review. It commented on the fact "that the probation service in Northern Ireland is understaffed, and that difficulties arise when female probationers have to be supervised by male probation officers". This proved to be a very comprehensive report which called for radical improvements in juvenile court constitution. It called for training for lay childrens magistrates; a clearer use of language for the sake of families and the compilation of straightforward leaflets explaining the nature of training school orders. A psychiatric service for training schools was recommended and attendance centres were advocated as an alternative provision to residential care. The inadequate accommodation in juvenile courts was decried and the urgent need for improvement emphasized. As for the age of criminal responsibility, it was recommended that this be raised up to twelve years of age on the grounds that offences involving young children were largely due to a lack of discipline and parental control and such children were more in need of care or control. However in spite of the conclusions to the contrary of "various associations in England", the Council Report maintained that the Juvenile Court should still be regarded as the best tribunal for dealing with children. The majority view of the Council was that there should be legal aid made available in all cases where representation was desired. A strong recommendation was also made that there should be a drive to recruit and train more probation officers.

B — SOCIAL WORK SEEKS AN IDENTITY

Training Needs are Reviewed

The shortage of trained social workers was reaching crisis point, not just in the probation service but nationally. Consequently a Government committee was set up to examine the question and to make recommendations. The Younghusband Committee reported in 1959: it was concerned only with staffing needs of Local Authority Departments.

The Committee tried to work from the basis of needs in the community and suggested three kinds of need: complex problems which required the skills of a trained and experienced social worker; more straightforward problems which nevertheless required a basic training in social work for those dealing with them, and routine problems could be dealt with by an untrained but mature member of staff working under the supervision of a trained social worker. These last-named members of staff were called "welfare assistants".

The Younghusband Committee recognized that a crash programme of training courses was going to be required to try to meet these staffing needs. Consequently they proposed a two year Certificate of Social Work to be taken at Colleges of Further Education. A Northern Ireland course was set up at the Rupert Stanley College of Further Education in 1964.

This left social work education in a rather chaotic state with three types of training available at this stage:

a two-year diploma in social studies, taken at university and accepted as a basic qualification in social work;
a postgraduate specialist training, also taken at University, in psychiatric social work, medical social work, child care, family casework or probation;
the new Certificate in Social Work.

Unfortunately from being a temporary expedient, the Certificate in Social Work became recognized as equivalent to a postgraduate university qualification. It has been argued by some that, as a result, social work qualifications were devalued rather than improved.[a]

---

[a] There are now several social work courses leading to the Certificate of Qualification in Social Work in Northern Ireland. These are at diploma, undergraduate and postgraduate levels and based in Queen's University Belfast (postgraduate), University of Ulster (postgraduate, undergraduate and diploma). As indicated in Chapter VI, an attempt is now being made to introduce a universal qualification in social work.

Towards a Comprehensive Welfare Service

At the same time as this professionalisation of social work was under way, Local Authority services continued to expand and improve in the following ways.

First of all, there was a diversifying of services. In other words a wider range of services became available to meet specific needs. For example: day-centres, sheltered dwellings, workshops, psychiatric hostels, rehabilitation centres, family group homes. There were interesting experiments in combining facilities, such as the grouping of old people's homes, day-centres and sheltered dwellings together. Secondly, attempts were made to provide a more specialist service. For instance, reception and assessment units, short-term admission units and emergency foster-care were introduced to complement existing children's homes. Thirdly decentralization was introduced to bring services closer to the community they served and to be more responsive to community needs. 'Divisional' offices as they were called soon developed 'sub-offices' and some of these developed their own roles, for example as family advice centres. Finally, administratively the wheel came full circle. In the early days welfare departments had appointed specialist officers. Thus one had "children's visitors", "home teachers for the blind", "visitors for the aged", "boarding-out officers" and so on. In the 1960s there was a move towards general "social welfare officers" who might be in contact with all client groups. However, with the increase in staffing there came a more complex administrative hierarchy and most senior posts remained specialist in nature, like the Home Help Organizer, Assistant Children's Officers, Principal Social Welfare Officer for Mental Health. An attempt was made to integrate other professions with relevant expertize, such as occupational therapists for work with the disabled.

These developments were not without their casualties and it was unfortunate that welfare assistants became identified with work with the elderly and the provision of the home help service rather than carrying out a full range of routine duties under the supervision of a qualified member of staff. The result was that elderly people in the main probably received a less professional service.

An extensive programme of staff training was embarked on and this led to the development of specifically "trainee" posts. Some of them also became specialist – for example, trainee social worker for the deaf.

The combination of fairly rapid organizational growth with turnover of staff going on courses obviously created acute problems. One was the lack of continuity of contact, for example, with boarded-out children, or with 'problem families'. Another was that staff returning from courses were promoted too quickly and so lost contact with clients.

Nevertheless, although there was substantial regional variation in the quantity and quality of services[b], there was considerable progress in this decade towards a comprehensive social welfare provision.

For example, a wide range of services were available to old people: home help, meals on wheels, luncheon clubs, a laundry service, night help service, adaptations to their own homes, aids to daily living, day-centres, holidays, sheltered dwellings, old people's homes, residential units for the confused, and as was mentioned earlier, combinations of these. There were imaginative experiments in the use of technology such as pre-cooked meals. The home help service was extended to include neighbourhood wardens and consideration was given to developing an inter-com system in the homes of old people at risk.

For the disabled, a strenuous attempt was made to recruit occupational therapists with their valuable expertise and a purpose-built assessment and rehabilitation centre was designed and built. The thinking behind it was perhaps too progressive and it assumed a degree of medical co-operation in the community which did not materialize. Services for the blind remained fairly static apart from the development of trained mobility officers. Professionalization helped services for the deaf, if only by highlighting deficiencies, such as the difficulties facing the hard-of-hearing school leaver. Nevertheless services continued to be provided in healthy co-operation with voluntary organizations concerned with the deaf.

In the field of child care there were also developments which illustrate increasing specialization and professionalism. These included progress in adoption, changing relationships and voluntary children's homes and new preventive powers under the Children and Young Persons Act (Northern Ireland) 1968.

The Basis for a Modern Adoption Service

The Child Welfare Council Report of 1963 "Adoption of Children" sets the tone.[20] The Hurst Committee had reported on adoption in England and Wales in 1954 to be followed by the Adoption Act of 1958. Certain features now characterized adoption practice in England and Wales which contrasted with Northern Ireland. For instance the Juvenile Courts had jurisdiction to make Adoption Orders there but not in Northern Ireland. There was more flexibility there concerning residence and domicile requirements for adoption applicants. An Adoption Order was usually made in a single hearing

---

[b] The authorities in the East of the Province, Antrim, Belfast and Down, have always had substantially better staffing and facilities. This was caused by social workers' own preferences and political priorities.

whereas two were required in Northern Ireland. And the guardian ad litem in England and Wales was a nominated individual usually from a Local Authority agency or probation department which was not directly involved in arrangements for the adoption – in Northern Ireland the guardian ad litem was usually also the welfare authority concerned in the placement arrangements.

The Council Report stated that in the period 1955–1959 there had been 1409 applications for adoption in Northern Ireland and 1267 Adoption Orders were made. Ninety-nine per cent of the children involved were under 5 years of age and more than 50% were under 2 years of age. Overall 53.6% were girls, although the proportion was much higher amongst the youngest children. There were only four adoption societies active at this time and only one employed a full-time fieldworker. Third party and direct placements accounted for 39% of the children placed between 1955 and 1960 and the Council recommended that more control over such placements was justifiable. There was also a suggestion that some social workers were reluctant to place second or additional illegitimate children of unmarried mothers or the illegitimate off-spring of married mothers as there might be some sort of taint of immorality which could be hereditary! It was urged that such a policy be discontinued in the interests of the children. Other recommendations included: that Interim Orders be retained but that normal practice should be for an adoption order to be made at a single hearing after three months continuous care and possession of the child by the adoption applicants (subject too to more supervisory powers being introduced to protect the child's interests); that the juvenile courts as they existed were not suitable to undertake adoption proceedings; that there should be more flexibility for applicants domiciled in Great Britain and resident in Northern Ireland, or vice versa; there was also a majority opinion that an independent Guardian ad litem should be appointed in all cases. Another interesting issue raised concerned the right of the adopted child to see his or her birth certificate. It was felt that because Northern Ireland was such a small community, easy access to such information could lead to all sorts of personal tragedies. Thus they concluded that the existing position should be retained whereby the Registrar General would only give information about an original birth certificate in exceptional circumstances and on the basis of an order from a court. It was felt that close links needed to be established between adoption societies and the voluntary homes.

In effect the Adoption Act (Northern Ireland) 1967 was drawn up largely in line with the recommendations of the Child Welfare Council Report. As a result adoption law and practice underwent a significant change, becoming much more closely aligned to the rest of the United Kingdom. Thus, for instance, the courts were empowered to make a final adoption order on the basis of a single hearing, if the applicants had had three months continuous care and possession of the child. More flexibility was also introduced in terms of residence qualifications by the provision that it would be sufficient if one spouse was resident in Northern Ireland for the three month period and both spouses had lived together for at least one of the three months. As protection of the interests of the child, it was confirmed in the Act that the welfare authority had to agree to the placement and would supervise the child until the adoption took place. If the child was not subsequently adopted, the welfare authority could, if in the interests of the child, take it into care. The suggestion that the guardian ad litem should be independent of adoption placement arrangements was not embodied in the Act.

A further Adoption Act was passed in England and Wales in 1968 which allowed courts to make Orders under the Hague Convention on adoption and giving recognition to certain overseas Adoption Orders. Northern Ireland followed suit by a further Adoption Act legalizing the Hague Convention in 1969.

The Continuing Role of Voluntary Children's Homes

A further report of the Child Welfare Council in 1966 on "The Role of the Voluntary Homes in the Child Care Service" gave an interesting historical perspective on the balance between voluntary and statutory provisions. [21] Up to 1950, the Children's Inspector appointed by the Ministry of Home Affairs would visit and inspect homes caring for poor children and young persons who were supported wholly or in part by voluntary contributions. There was no power at this stage to require registration and the Ministry had no authority in the decisions concerning the lives of the children. With the Children and Young Persons Act (Northern Ireland) 1950 and the Voluntary Homes Regulations 1952 came the first requirements in relation to registration and inspection and the controls over maximum numbers to be accommodated.

The continuing role of the voluntary homes was reflected in the statistics of children in their care as at 31 March 1965. There were 822 children in 20 voluntary homes, 238 of whom were in the care of the welfare authorities. The 20 homes sub-divided as follows:

12	homes	organized by Roman Catholic religious orders
3	homes	organized by three Protestant denominations
4	homes	with a strong religious background
1	home	of purely secular origin.

At the same time the welfare authorities were providing for 1195 children in their own forms of care. Only 16% of children who were the sole responsibility of the voluntary organizations were boarded-out in foster homes compared with 54% of the children in the care of welfare authorities.

There was a strong call from the Council for all voluntary organizations to employ more qualified workers. Indeed the staff ratios were often adjudged to be insufficient to meet the individual needs of children in residential care (ie rising above a ratio of 1:6). It was also felt that co-ordination between welfare authorities and voluntary organizations, especially Roman Catholic Homes, still left a lot to be desired, and it was suggested that people should be employed in welfare authorities with specific responsibilities for liaison with voluntary groups.

The Introduction of Preventive Child Care

As well as the growing emphasis on the need for recruitment and training of staff and co-ordination of services, there was also an argument that social services for families were similar to the manning of ambulances at the foot of cliffs. In other words they responded to crises and applied bandages after the accidents. The outcome of the call for preventive social work in England and Wales which would enable social workers to anticipate crises in families had led to the Children and Young Persons Act of 1963. This Act gave Local Authorities the discretionary power to assist families materially or with cash payments where it was clear that to do so would reduce the need to bring children into care or to bring them before juvenile courts. In due course the Children and Young Persons Act (Northern Ireland) 1968 became law. This re-enacted the 1950 Act with amendments which echoed closed provisions within the 1963 Act in England and Wales. Section 164 virtually transposed the preventive section of the 1963 Act verbatim and the guidelines for effecting it were very similar to those of the English Home Office at an earlier stage. The point was made that the discretionary power to give assistance should not be used as a sort of extended arm of the Supplementary Benefits Commission. In practice this section has come under much criticism since its conception on the grounds that it is a discretionary power open to all sorts of interpretation with no really consistent criteria. It is also, unlike decisions about levels of supplementary benefits, not open to an appeal by the client. These criticisms have been particularly trenchant on the part of some social workers themselves working with families who are struggling on or below the poverty line in the face of a cost of living which rates as one of the highest in the British Isles. On the other hand, another aspect of this section which is perhaps under-used is that relating to assistance to families as a means of diminishing the need to keep children in care. This had a strong positive rehabilitative flavour and was open to imaginative use by social workers in the interest of families.

As another aspect of preventive work, Section 163 provided that "where, in consequence of any investigation arising out of the alleged commission of an offence, a member of the Royal Ulster Constabulary is of the opinion that a child or young person may be in need of advice, guidance or assistance for any reason and is not to be brought before a court it shall be his duty to notify the welfare authority (Health and Social Services Board)". Social services departments entered into discussions with the RUC to work out the best methods of implementing this section. In practice, at least in the early stages, some RUC personnel appeared to regard social workers as a source of information to help them make up their minds *whether* they should bring a child to court or not – in other words, to judge whether children were deserving of leniency or not.

In the 1968 Act a number of situations are identified in which children and young persons are potentially vulnerable and it outlines what should be acceptable practice and procedures. There is an underlying assumption that while the state has a responsibility for supervision and regulation, parents retain the responsibility to make provision for the physical, mental and moral welfare of their children. With the exception of the prevention section outlined above, the Act does not accommodate any of the more sweeping changes advocated in the Kilbrandon Report of 1964 and subsequent Social Work (Scotland) Act of 1968 or the two White Papers in England and Wales, "The Child, the Family and the Young Offender" (1965) and "Children in Trouble" (1968), the latter influencing the Children and Young Persons Act 1969. It is rather a consolidation of the principles underlying previous children's legislation. Thus the Juvenile Court remained the judicial forum in which any statutory intervention into the lives of children and young persons took place and the distinction was maintained between offenders and non-offenders. On the other hand prevention became a central policy and heavy emphasis was placed on proper regard being made to the welfare of the child.

The recommendation of the Child Welfare Council in the Report of 1960 on "The Operation of Juvenile Courts in Northern Ireland" that the age of criminal responsibility be raised to 12 years of age was not adopted. Instead, 10 years of age was determined as the age of criminal responsibility and between the ages of 10 and 14 years a child was presumed not to have the capacity to commit a criminal act unless it could be proved that at the time he committed the act he knew it was wrong (the "doli incapax" presumption).

Modifications were made to the provisions relating to children in need of care, protection or control. The "double test" contained in the 1950 Act was retained but the former requirement to prove that a parent was "unfit" to care for a child was substituted by a requirement to show that the parent was not acting as "a good parent" should the latter being a somewhat easier case to establish. In addition to the other provisions any of which needed to be fulfilled for a child to be defined in need of care and protection (namely, falling into bad associations, exposed to moral danger, Schedule I offences committed), it was now made possible to demonstrate a need for care and protection by establishing that: "the lack of care, protection or guidance is likely to cause him unnecessary suffering or seriously affect his health or proper development". (Sec 93(i) b(ii).)

The 1968 Act also provided extensive requirements for private fostering – where children are placed in care of someone other than a relative (unless less than a month during school holidays). Following notification of such arrangements, the Welfare Authority (from October 1973 the Area Board) had to give consent or notice of withholding consent in writing to the person receiving and the person handing over the child. The Authority was also required to visit from time to time in such cases to ensure that proper care was being given and to give advice concerning the welfare of the child. The Welfare Authority had the power, if any child was found to be improperly kept, to remove him to a place of safety by Court Order, or in an emergency, by an Order made by a Justice of the Peace.

Equally wide-ranging regulations were introduced in relation to childminding — where a child is looked after for more than two hours in the day on more than two occasions in the week. Registration of premises by the Welfare Authority became compulsory and requirements could be imposed in relation to such issues as the number of children cared for, records, staffing, medical facilities. These registers were to be made available for public inspection.

A formal and expanding register of dayminding arrangements was welcomed by many professional social workers as a potential broadening of community resources for families in need of support. It is probably accurate to say however that in spite of some publicity, this area of child care in Northern Ireland has remained relatively under-developed.

What proved to be the final report of the Child Welfare Council emerged in 1969, its brief being to consider the terms of the Children and Young Persons Boarding Out Regulations of 1950.[22] Many constructive recommendations resulted which were to have a significant influence on the revised Boarding-out Regulations of 1976. Two issues were perhaps of particular historical significance. The Council noted that up to this point there had been no statutory regulations aimed specifically at the protection of children boarded-out from voluntary homes apart from the general provisions of Part I of the Children and Young Persons Act (Northern Ireland) 1968. The 1976 Boarding-Out Regulations were in fact to introduce regulations concerning children boarded-out by voluntary organizations, including the general duty allotted to Area Boards to satisfy themselves that any organization boarding out children in their area was in fact in a position to discharge those supervisory duties satisfactorily. If not, the Boards were given the power subject to representations, to take over and perform those duties. It would appear however that the mutual antagonism and suspicion between the statutory and certain voluntary child care organizations has once again been in evidence on this issue and further clarification of the legal functions and rights of the various parties may be required in future legislation.

A further issue considered by the Council was concerning Regulation 4 of the 1950 Regulations which required reports on children not boarded-out after three months of being received into care to be forwarded to the Ministry of Home Affairs. It was postulated that this regulation no longer served any useful purpose as the time had arrived "when reliance can be placed upon welfare authorities to act in this matter in the best interests of the child". This conclusion was also arrived at on the basis that Section 114 of the Children and Young Persons Act (Northern Ireland) 1968 adequately stressed the desirability of boarding out where "practical and desirable". In the event, the Boarding-Out Regulations of 1976 were to omit the old 1950 requirement to notify the Ministry. It is also interesting to note however, that in the primary legislation of England and Wales there had been a similar emphasis on fostering which was to be repealed in the 1969 Children and Young Persons Act. One of the arguments in favour of this change from the social work practice viewpoint, was that it should be a professional decision as to which forms of care best met the needs of individual children. There undoubtedly remains a question as to whether the legal direction concerning boarding out which is still implicit in the Children and Young Persons Act (Northern Ireland) 1968 should be repealed in future legislation. Fostering has proved to be far from a panacea for all children and indeed British research studies have indicated that there can be quite a high risk of breakdown if careful assessment and practice is not carried out. In addition, with the modern purpose-built residential homes established and planned and a growing number of trained staff in Northern Ireland, it is important to recognize and cultivate the potential strengths of residential child care in meeting the needs of at least certain children.

Advances in Mental Health Legislation

The progressive aspects of the 1948 Mental Health Act in the field of mental health were further developed by the Mental Health Act (Northern Ireland) 1961. A strong emphasis on community care had been placed by the Royal Commission on Mental Illness in 1957 which preceded the corresponding English Act. In addition, the thinking of the Commission had been conditioned by the revolution in drug treatment in the 1950s.

There were several major changes in the 1961 Act. Psychiatric treatment was to be made available on the same basis as treatment for physical illness, including receiving treatment in general hospital. In line with this, 'certification' and 'temporary treatment' were replaced by 'formal admission' (against the patient's wishes where treatment was thought necessary in the interests of the patient or those around him/her). The judicial aspect was removed and responsibility placed with relatives or, in their absence, the social worker. The period of detention was strictly limited to 21 days (7 days in the case of an emergency admission) although there were provisions to extend this in certain cases. Patients had the right to appeal to the Mental Health Review Tribunal, a judicial body having power to discharge or reclassify a patient.

The 1961 Northern Ireland Mental Health Act retained the lead which local legislation had over that in England and Wales. The word 'mental' was mostly replaced by 'psychiatric' and indeed was dropped altogether from the name of the Department for the Affairs of (Mental) Patients which had responsibility for patients' property. The concept (and terminology) of "in need of special care" was retained and the Northern Ireland Act managed to avoid the thorny issues of 'psychopathy'. The responsibility of relatives was recognized and there was less scope for direct intervention by the 'Mental Welfare Officer' – an unknown breed in Northern Ireland.

On the other hand, the notion of hospital treatment (provided by the Hospitals Authority) continued to predominate and community services were slow to develop. One exception was County Down which pioneered an imaginative scheme of psychiatric hostels run in co-operation with the local psychiatric hospital.

It remained true that specialist community workshops and specialist hostels were underdeveloped. There was little sign of the idea of providing psychiatric services through the district general hospital being taken seriously.

Training and Probation

Recognition of the need for training and staff development in the probation service was evidenced by the appointment in 1966 of a senior probation officer specifically responsible for in-service training. In the same year the first probation officer with a professional social work qualification was appointed. The following year saw the seconding of the first probation officer on to a professional training course. This marked the beginning of a new era of recruitment and training and a growing concern among the staff of the probation service to establish a professional identity. The fact that the Rainer House course in England (which did not carry a professional qualification) became closed to Northern Ireland probation officers from 1968 only acted as a spur to develop a recruitment and secondment policy. By 1972 there were 46 probation officers in post, which was in effect double the number in post in 1966. And the newly created post of "trainee probation officer" was introduced, which helped to widen the recruitment net.[23]

In 1967 a probation officer was seconded to Belfast prison as the first official prison welfare officer. With the Treatment of Offenders Act 1968, the Northern Ireland probation service took on responsibility for the statutory after-care of certain categories of offenders on release from prison. Between 1969 and 1974 the number of prison welfare officers in the Prison Welfare Service increased from one individual to nine with one senior officer. This reflected the growing needs of a prison population which had increased five-fold during the same period. (In 1974 there was a suspension of statutory licensing, and from that time the involvement of probation officers with prisoners after release was mainly on a voluntary basis). It has been suggested that the drive to develop welfare units in prisons was to some extent to the detriment of other aspects of the service. Be that as it may the prison welfare officers are now represented in Crumlin Road Prison, Belfast; the Maze Prison, Hillsborough; Magilligan near Limavady and Armagh Women's Prison. Each prison has a welfare department staffed by probation officers seconded to the prison setting, usually on a 2 year basis.

In spite of the real progress made in this decade, there were still some obvious gaps in provision. Homeless single persons, particularly women, were scarcely catered for. Although services for discharged psychiatric patients were developing there was an inadequate range of services, for example graded workshops in the community, special units for alcoholics. Services for the mentally handicapped remained the responsibility of the Special Care Authority, an adjunct of the Hospitals Authority and facilities were mostly institutional. Equally, the Education Welfare Service, which was the responsibility of the Education Department, failed to professionalize and remained bedevilled by the outdated ethos of the School Attendance Officer.

Nevertheless, the decade was a remarkably forward-looking one with the hospitals building on the firm foundation of professional social work, welfare departments developing increasing expertise, the probation service expanding, and voluntary organizations such as Barnardo's, the NSPCC and the Belfast Council of Social Welfare adding to their prestigious record of family casework.

C — SOCIAL WORK IN THE 'TROUBLES'

Two developments unfortunately put all this achievement into the melting pot: one was the civil disturbances which began in earnest in August 1969; the other was the major structural re-organization of health and social services which took place in October 1973.

Welfare and Bureaucracy

The 'troubles' of 1969 and succeeding years are often spoken of as if they were an entity, yet the tactics which terrorists adopted were constantly changing and these changes created new problems for social workers. The difficulties were compounded by inconsistencies both at Westminster and at Stormont (before it was dissolved).

From the social services point of view the events appeared as a series of waves of violence with lulls in between. Even this only applies to the earlier disturbances because at a later stage (for example 1972), there was insidious continuing intimidation of individual families.

To give some idea of the complexity of events, at least nine different kinds of disturbance can be distinguished.

1. There were the first riots of August 1969 when a large number of families left their homes. Some were burnt out; others left temporarily and returned to find their homes destroyed; others left in panic and returned the next day; others left perfectly good homes because they were too frightened to live in the area.

   The sheer size of the task in keeping track of this situation, let alone dealing with it can be imagined.

   Added to this were problems for social workers 'on the ground'. For example, there was simply the question of physical access with many side streets barricaded off by paving stones. There was also the problem of suspicion. Thirdly, there was a real communication problem. New decisions were taken daily and new schemes brought into operation – for example, to provide immediate financial assistance. Social workers on the ground were not always aware of these.

   These riots continued to have repercussions for the following year as temporary housing sites were set up and re-housing proceeded on a large scale.

2. The second 'wave' was the 'evacuation' of a Protestant housing estate in West Belfast at Easter 1970. This was almost certainly a political manoeuvre which misfired. Panic was started that there was to be a confrontation between the Protestant and Catholic communities and Protestant women and children were moved out to the safety of a school on the Shankill Road. This was the first example of families leaving home voluntarily for political ends.

3. In June 1970 there were riots in East Belfast and Catholic families moved into a Catholic enclave around St Matthews Church.

   The incident illustrated the change in official attitudes towards families

page 103

leaving their homes, which was an increasingly hard one.

1970 was the year of the 'hearts and minds' battle in which the IRA were trying to make capital out of the "British Army" as an "army of occupation" while central Government wished to portray them as allies and protectors. Riots therefore created a dilemma for Government, since they had to be quelled, yet efforts at quelling them could be seen as brutal repression.

Central Government also became aware that emergency supplies supposedly being made available to families were in fact being channelled to the provisional IRA. Consequently attitudes hardened and families who left their homes voluntarily were told they could expect no help. Social workers, of course, were in the front line of this particular battle.

4. Ironically, there was extensive flooding in Belfast on the night of 15 August 1970 – the first anniversary of the 'troubles'. This at least gave the Army the opportunity to show themselves as 'on the community's side'. Social workers were again asked to carry out quite exceptional duties: making sure that carpets were dried out; arranging the supply of hot meals; carrying out surveys of affected areas. Again, they were in the front line and if there were delays by other corporation departments (for example, the Public Health Department or the City Surveyor's Department) it was the social workers who were blamed.

Healthily enough, local communities had learnt the value of peaceful street protest and certain roads were blocked by tenants who felt that not enough was being done.

5. 1971 saw a further change in tactics, away from rioting and the large-scale movement of families towards the use of car-bombs. Originally these were directed at commercial premises in the centre of Belfast but they soon moved to residential areas. Pubs were a popular target and in the process private homes were obviously also damaged.

This again posed a different set of problems for social workers – for example, personal safety was more of an issue. However, they were in a sense easier to deal with because one could more readily tap voluntary resources in the neighbourhood.

6. The Twelfth of July celebrations each year were obviously a sensitive point and they were now being succeeded by a series of anniversaries. It was hardly surprising therefore that trouble flared again in August 1972 in which once more several streets of houses in Ardoyne, a working-class area in North Belfast, were burnt down.

Welfare and Bureaucracy

This incident differed from earlier ones in that it seemed that Protestant families had voluntarily left their homes, mostly moving to houses in Protestant estates which had gradually been vacated by Catholic families. It appeared that the families had deliberately destroyed their earlier homes to make sure that they would not be taken over by Catholic families.

Once again political capital was made out of the incident and if attempts were made to tailor services to needs, there was the actual risk of being branded a "Catholic lover".

Fuel was added to the flames by the introduction of internment at this time.

7. During 1973 terrorist tactics took another turn. There were a series of assassinations, some of them apparently quite indiscriminate.

   During all this time, insidious intimidation of individual families was going on; and bit by bit the two communities became completely polarized geographically.

   In terms of the scale of the problem, this was easier to deal with, but it brought with it ethical problems, for example, how far support might be given to a family who did not wish to leave their area but who might be under threat from extremists. This kind of conflict also created many short-term psychological problems.

8. The introduction of internment was soon followed by the peaceful protest of an extensive rent and rates strike. This was countered by a most repressive piece of legislation, the Payment for Debt (Emergency Provisions) Act, Northern Ireland 1971. Yet again social workers were caught between clients in hardship and regulations over which they had no control.

   Although the Act was designed to deal with those voluntarily withholding rent and rates, it inevitably extended to vulnerable groups who had genuine difficulty in meeting their commitments because of a low, fixed income, such as pensioners. The implementation of such a measure shows to what extent central Government attitudes had changed since 1969.

9. The demise of Stormont and the introduction of Direct Rule brought its own problems, some of which found expression in the test of strength of the Ulster Workers' Council strike.

   This was completely different from earlier incidents because it was a controlled strike. Consequently there was plenty of prior warning and steps could be taken to ensure that vulnerable groups did not suffer. Furthermore, social workers had by now developed considerable expertise in dealing with emergencies.

A Service for People

There were important lessons to be learnt from these disturbances. The kind of organizational requirements they posed included:
speed of response, because events moved so quickly;
open-mindedness: not to assume that each incident was a replica of the preceding one;
devolution: local decision-making, because individual needs were different in each case;
maximum use of local resources with minimum central control; trust;
good communication: this assumes a clear organizational structure and ideally a small group of people working together who know each other well.

These requirements could not be more different from the bureaucratic methods of central Government. If one reviews each of them in turn:

The unwieldy Civil Service machinery of central Government is not noted for speed of response. For example, it took several months to persuade the Supplementary Benefit Commission of the value of accessible local offices.

Inflexibility is another deep-rooted aspect of bureaucracy and central Government was very concerned to treat each incident as if it resembled the previous one. If policy was changed to suit the second one, this same policy would then inappropriately be applied to the third.

Central Government by definition depends on centralization. This caused innumerable delays because inquiries would have to be passed from clients through the welfare department to central Government and down again.

The use of local resources was hampered throughout by central Government's wish to continue to exercise control.

The issue of trust was a very big problem. Welfare departments mistrusted central Government and vice versa (because welfare departments were Unionist controlled), voluntary organizations mistrusted statutory departments. In particular, the Catholic community mistrusted the statutory services (because they felt they had been ill-done by in the past, for example in employment and housing).

There was no clear structure of authority. Central Government adhered to its policy of 'power without responsibility' and welfare department social workers were left with the responsibility of providing services without the power of controlling resources.

In spite of these serious organizational deficiencies there were positive aspects to the disturbances. Most importantly, they revealed very powerful forces towards self-help in local communities and these years saw an unparalleled mushrooming of community activities.

They also, for a short time, brought certain statutory departments in close contact, notably the housing department, the welfare department and the supplementary benefits commission. These contacts undoubtedly led to a greater understanding of shared problems and carried over into normal working relationships, at least until the reorganization of the health and social services in October 1973.

Central Government was unable to harness these powerful forces. Their ambivalent attitude towards self-help is clearly illustrated in the short and chequered history of the Community Relations Commission. This was set up in December 1969 under the Community Relations Act (Northern Ireland) 1969 with the politically naive view at the time that such a body might help to bring the two communities together although each was clearly set on creating a kind of apartheid. Although the Commission was supposed to act as an independent body which might help to articulate local public opinion by encouraging and developing community groups, central Government made sure that the new organization had no teeth by vesting financial control of grant aid in a separate Ministry of Community Relations. The platitudes and good intentions voiced in the Ministry's first report ("There is another way ...") would be comical when read against the background of subsequent events were it not for the sombreness of those events.

In practice, the Commission embarked on a progressive programme of staff development and through it, aimed at the province-wide encouragement of community development. Their handling of the emergency surrounding the introduction of internment was a model of public relations in the best sense of the term.

Sadly, the rest of their brief history was a series of wrangles with their own Ministry, mainly about the appropriate use of scarce resources. There were resignations and the Commission disintegrated. It was with some relief that the Ministry of Health and Social Services, which had acted as midwife in 1969, placed the troublesome toddler in the care of the Department of Education in 1974.

The Role of the Probation Officer

The probation service too experienced difficulties at this time since some of the legislation passed to deal with civil disturbances also had the effect of causing confusion about the probation officer's role in the courts. In 1970, for instance, the Criminal Justice (Temporary Provisions) Act (Northern Ireland) provided for the imposition of minimum sentences of imprisonment for certain offences during the so-called "emergency" situation. It outlined a list of "scheduled offences" attaching a

A Service for People

minimum custodial period. Any person convicted of these offences was to be sentenced to not less than the prescribed period regardless of anything to the contrary in any other statutory provision. This meant in effect that minimal sentences ranged from six months in the case of a person convicted of riotous or disorderly behaviour and breach of the peace to 5 years for an offence under Section 2 of the Explosive Substances Act 1875. It was applied in blanket fashion to juveniles but the Juvenile Court did not waive the requirement on the probation service to supply reports – even though there was now no discretion as to the decisions about disposal. As a result probation officers were being asked to gather information on the social background of offenders where from the outset it was known that a statutory institutional sentence would be imposed. There was a further amending Act in 1970 but even with this, any young person over the age of fourteen years would be subject to some form of detention. In other words, the principles which underpinned the Children and Young Persons' legislation in Northern Ireland in relation to "the welfare of the child" no longer applied in such cases. With home visits becoming at times difficult if not impossible and dangerous, there were occasions when social enquiry reports were being completed with families in the court building on the day of the hearing. In effect such reports were lists of information rather than any real appraisal of the situation.

Not surprisingly, the probation service was concerned that the officers' involvement could be viewed as giving an official stamp to a completely re-arranged process. This proved to be a troubled and difficult time for the probation service.

In 1973 the Emergency Provisions Act abolished mandatory sentences and established special courts with one judge assuming the responsibility of the jury. These special courts began to deal with offences which had political or sectarian motivation. Some probation officers were reluctant to provide a service for these courts because they felt that the defendants only had limited rights in the process. On the other hand, some officers argued that at least they could now make their assessments on an objective basis and have it properly considered by a court before decisions were reached about disposal. This was seen as an important professional social work task reflecting the defendant's needs which would otherwise be neglected or overlooked, even where the offence had a political or sectarian motivation. Balanced against this were the real fears that the collaboration with providing social enquiry reports could be seen to be involving the probation service in a political judgement. One senior probation officer explained his own feelings on this dilemma:

> "As probation officers, we accept that we are to some extent agents of social control and are attempting to modify the behaviour and attitudes of individuals and their families in their social situation through the use of social work skills and

techniques. These skills and techniques are not tools for attempting to modify political motivation, attitudes or behaviour. Probation officers are agents of social control — they are not agents of political control."

Nonetheless such issues have subjected the probation officers to a series of ethical crises which in many respects are still being resolved. On a more pragmatic level, the last few years have caused probation officers to reflect on how acceptable their service is in certain neighbourhoods in the Province because of a lack of trust in their roles.

Alongside the political and ethical issues, the Northern Ireland probation service was looking at the merits of a community service scheme for certain offenders as an alternative to prison. Breidge Dolan, described the background preparation for the scheme in Northern Ireland[24]:

> "In May 1975 as a result of a conference on "Alternatives to Prison"... a study group was set up to look at the possibility of Community Service Orders in Northern Ireland. The group now operates under the official title of "Extern" and has broadened its outlook to include the setting up of hostels for the offender in Northern Ireland. The group (including University staff, probation officers, community and voluntary workers, trade union representatives and residential staff), felt that the ordinary offender in Northern Ireland tended to be neglected by our society both inside and outside of prison, largely because of everyone's pre-occupation with the "Troubles". New and exciting methods are being introduced in England and Wales dealing with the offender, yet we do not even give them serious consideration because of our often mistaken conviction that they could not possibly work here."

Breidge Dolan asserted that the troubled situation in the Province should add impetus to such an initiative, as opposed to being an impossible drawback! "There is no doubt that, as a result of our situation in Northern Ireland, communities have been forced to group together to provide 'self-help'. The result of this has been an awareness of all problems and a desire to offer help from within the community – in many ways an ideal situation for the successful operation of community service orders". Indeed she pointed out that voluntary agencies such as the Voluntary Services Bureau, Playground Schemes, Youth Clubs, Tenants' Associations, Clubs for the Handicapped, had all expressed a positive wish to be involved with CSO projects. The Treatment of Offenders (Northern Ireland) Order 1976 allowed courts to make community service orders and to defer sentence. As a result of this, a senior probation officer was appointed to take charge of a Community Service Unit in the Belfast area, with the initial objective of making contact with the various voluntary and statutory agencies and create a basis for the new venture.

Violence and Social Work

Since the civil disturbances began in 1969, there has been a wide variation in levels of violence in different parts of the Province. Clearly the most affected areas in the Province are North and West Belfast, where there are innumerable flashpoints, coupled with unemployment rates that rise to nearly 40% in some districts. It is here that the effects of violence are most vividly seen, be it in the lack of amenities such as regular bus services or cinemas or the presence of Army encampments. J Darby and A Williamson emphasize however that "the disease may be most obviously present in North and West Belfast, but the symptoms are everywhere."[25] They also usefully identify some of the major issues which violence has caused for the personal social services. Because of imprisonment, threats of hospitalization through injury, the number of one-parent families increased. Through involvement in rioting and disorders, more young children were at risk. Outlying towns such as Craigavon, Antrim and Lisburn began to receive evacuees from Belfast and this added to the number of one-parent families, physically handicapped, psychologically disturbed and socially isolated in these areas. By its very nature, violence tested out the validity of social workers using traditional casework models of practice which were more appropriate to more stable societies.

Darby and Williamson also assert somewhat contentiously that, in the immediate period after violence had erupted, Antrim and Down Welfare Authorities responded in a flexible and committed manner whilst Belfast Welfare Authority was reluctant to accept that the social upheaval was within its remit until compelled by Government to take special measures. As has been indicated earlier, the welfare officers within Belfast were having to work extraordinarily long hours in many instances in the face of bureaucratic frustrations at all levels and ambivalent attitudes amongst the elected representatives of the Welfare Committee. A lack of clarity in their role was evident as often they were attempting to carry out both casework and civil defence functions, and perhaps succeeding at neither.

Viewing the wider issue of the relationship between violence and social work in Northern Ireland, there appears to be substantial truth in the suggestion of Darby and Williamson that many workers are reluctant to address the question at all. Alternatively it tends to be compartmentalized and not confronted as the pervasive influence that it is. As they put it: "In the main social casework in Northern Ireland continues along its traditional path and violence is regarded as an additional irritant rather than a catalyst". Our own view is that a proper analysis of violence and the role of the personal social services still needs to be confronted. The challenge is one that needs to be taken up, not just by practitioners, but at the level of social work training courses as well.

D — THE RE-STRUCTURING OF THE SOCIAL SERVICES

With characteristic aplomb, while these traumatic events were continuing, plans were proceeding to re-organize health and social services in Northern Ireland. This of course ran parallel to similar plans in Scotland, England and Wales. The method adopted was a national one too: to employ a firm of management consultants, rather on the American model, to review existing arrangements and suggest alternative new structures. This was duly done, with all the requisite jargon about 'input/throughput/output', ' delivery of services', 'monitoring', 'feedback' and so on.

Compared with earlier, humane reports (which of course is an unfair comparison) their findings appeared excessively mechanistic. They confined themselves to surveying the services currently available and made no attempt to ascertain the possible need for services. In other words, their brief was really to rationalize existing services and to suggest alternative ways of working. This they certainly did in a very methodical way. Unfortunately, they made certain basic assumptions which were not necessarily tenable. One was that there was a pool of qualified, open-minded managers available who could understand and apply the quite sophisticated management concepts and methods they proposed. Another was that there was a level of maturity both among the professions involved (medical, administrative, nursing, social work and so on) and within individual professions such that corporate management was feasible. Yet another, not made explicit, was that the historical timing was right for such major changes. The absence of historical and political commentary, even in passing, in the report is notable. There was also the assumption that re-organization was acceptable in good faith and not just, for example, as a take-over bid by hospitals, who after all had benefited most from the post-war expenditure.

The management consultants made far reaching proposals which included the dissolution of the distinction between hospitals and community care. In addition introduction of the concept of 'programmes of care' to ensure greater continuity of care was advocated. As programmes of care had to involve several professions they proposed that services should be planned and organized by means of corporate management, by democratic decision-making and not by a hierarchical autocracy. Furthermore, to avoid hierarchical decision making, programme planning teams were to have representatives of different grades of staff as well as different professional groups; in other words they should have horizontal (across professional groups) and vertical (across grades of seniority) representation. Considerable emphasis was placed on 'monitoring' activities, so that even after a programme of care was put into operation, the programme planning team would have a responsibility to review its progress. Finally, and the weakest aspect of the proposals, reference was made to 'consumer' representation through District Committees, but they were allocated no executive function.

Only the broad administrative framework of these proposals appeared in the Health and Personal Social Services (Northern Ireland) Order 1972. This was essentially a consolidating act and added little which was new as regards the provision of services.

The function of hospitals and special care authorities and of Local Authority Health and welfare departments were transferred to four Health and Personal Social Services Boards which were to be responsible for the full range of services: hospital, general practitioner, dental, community health and personal social services. (Thus medical social workers who had hitherto been employed by Hospital Management Committees were integrated under District Health & Social Services management.)

As has already been mentioned, from a social services point of view, little new was added. Although there was an apparently wider scope given "to promote the social welfare of the people of Northern Ireland", in actual practice individual sections dealt with "persons in need" and they were defined along the lines of the welfare services acts as the elderly, the physically handicapped, the mentally disordered, children and so on. There was a slight extension of services in that the Health and Personal Social Services Board might give financial assistance to a person in need "in exceptional circumstances constituting an emergency". The Ministry also had powers to register common lodging houses which were defined, rather quaintly for 1972 as "a house... provided for the purpose of accommodating by night poor persons".

The goals of re-organization (to rationalize services with a view to improving the quality of service and to make it more cost-effective) and the methods proposed were reasonable enough, but the assumptions on which they were based proved to be incorrect. The first problem was the imbalance between hospital and community services. Hospitals had grown inordinately and had been allowed to outstrip community provision. Consequently the risk was that instead of a partnership and indeed a merger, hospitals would simply absorb community services. There is no doubt that the geographical form of the final administrative structure was dictated by the Hospital Plan. Belfast provided the biggest headache because it had two major teaching hospitals in the Royal Victoria Hospital and the City Hospital. It also had a small hospital which was formerly a voluntary hospital (the Mater) and a new hospital which had been designed before re-organization was considered (the Ulster). In addition, it had one large psychiatric hospital (Purdysburn) and was also the regional centre for certain specialities, for example orthopaedics (at Musgrave Park Hospital) and child psychiatry. A compromise was reached by trying to integrate Belfast and County Down with one Health and Social Services Board, a solution which made the population:hospital ratio look reasonable on paper but which was socially ridiculous. Even within Belfast the areas of highest social need (and the loci of the worst of the disturbances — North and West Belfast) were also integrated into one unmanageable unit with the Royal Victoria Hospital as its district general hospital and the Mater as a poor relation.

The management consultants had wisely left the employment structure below posts of District Social Services Officers to be completed by the Area Boards themselves. In practice, District Social Services Officers were given complete autonomy and what in effect happened was that instead of four area boards there were seventeen districts, each competing for staff and resources. Empire-building took place on a vast scale and a large number of intermediary posts were created with no job description, role specification or attempt at management structuring. For example, where previously there had been two stages of communication between social worker and Divisional welfare officer, this was replaced by a possible seven:

District Social Services Officer
Principal Social Worker
Assistant Principal Social Worker (eg residential and daycare services)
Senior Social Worker (eg residential and daycare services)
Social Worker (District Headquarters, eg Adoption)
Assistant Principal Social Worker (Sub District)
Senior Social Worker (Sub District)
Social Worker.

This mushrooming of intermediary staff had several implications apart from managerial unwieldiness. Programmes of care became lost in the process because each profession — particularly social work — seemed intent on fortifying its own position. Even if programme planning teams had been in existence, horizontal and vertical representation became unworkable because of the numbers involved. More seriously, the turnover of staff going on courses and greatly increased opportunities for rapid promotion led to a 'flight from the client'. Welfare departments had traditionally to try to deal with the most deprived, least adequate members of the community. They were essentially a 'last ditch' service since there were few other organizations (apart from some voluntary ones like the Salvation Army and the Simon Community) to which clients could be passed on. Training emphasized the traditional casework approach which had largely been developed with middle-class clients in settings like child guidance.

This combination of intractable problems with inappropriate training and inadequate resources led to great frustrations. The support of the smaller, more personal welfare departments helped to some extent but with re-organization, it was as if working with clients was a chore to be tolerated for one or two years, with the promise of 'promotion' to an administrative post as the reward. If this is thought to be pure theory, let one consider the absence of any attempt to introduce a career structure for social workers who wished to work with clients and the fact that so-called social administrators tended to shy away from practical duties, such as participating in the duty rota. (In welfare departments, the duty rota was the exclusive responsibility of principal social workers and Divisional Welfare Officers).

Re-organization also raised wider issues. There are few who would deny that the old system based on welfare committees composed of elected councillors had many drawbacks. It is beyond dispute that many representatives were elected on extremely low polls, that vested interest was often present, and that the level of knowledge on many subjects was noticeably lacking. Nonetheless it was also abundantly in evidence that there were many public representatives with tremendous industry and unbiased social awareness who more than did justice to the democratic process. In any event, it is clear that the administrative structure on which the personal social services are now based has moved drastically from democratic to meritocratic assumptions. In other words, we appear to have "progressed" to an era where the "professional" feels that he can prescribe for people's needs with the minimum of accountability to the people for decisions taken. Indeed the issue of public accountability appears to be viewed as a rather irritating obsolete notion by many administrators of the health and personal social services. Ironically there is also the possibility that, having created this complex structure with its all-devouring administration, the Area Boards have decreased the likelihood of professional social workers being able to make cogent decisions! There is growing evidence that the goals in the social services are becoming more and more displaced away from "service to the community". We are now in an age of meetings, working parties and administrative complexities of the most absurd proportions — an unending variety of devices to divert energy and skill away from caring functions towards the self-perpetuating and self-justifying tasks which are commonly associated with the worst of mechanistic bureaucracies.

The Probation Service is Reviewed

During this period, the situation of the probation service vis-a-vis other professional social work was left in abeyance. Two Inspectors from the Home Office Probation Inspectorate presented a report on the Northern Ireland probation service in June 1973. Given that it must have been difficult to link into the specific situation in the Province, this appears to have been a constructive report. It recommended a review of the structure of the service and suggested that the option of integration with the personal social services should be closely examined. As an interim measure, the Ministry of

Home Affairs reconstructed the senior management hierarchy – a move interpreted in some quarters as the first real step in accepting proper responsibility for the service. (The Northern Ireland Office assumed responsibility for the service in 1974 following the proroguing of the Stormont Parliament although in effect the Civil Service team involved remained unchanged.)

There was to be a further review of the probation service by the Northern Ireland Social Work Advisory Group, the team based in the Department of Health and Social Services, in October 1976. Their report recommended that the Chief probation officer should be given more autonomy for decision-making. It encouraged the extension of the management hierarchy to develop training, research, planning and prison welfare with the emphasis on detailed fact-finding on which to base long-term decisions. There were 64 probation officers in post with 23 seconded on professional training courses, and it was envisaged that 40 more officers would be recruited by 1980. (This is perhaps put into a wider perspective when it is considered that Liverpool City had 200 probation officers in post in 1974.)

CHAPTER III
References

1. Seed, P (1973), *The Expansion of Social Work in Britain*, Routledge & Kegan Paul.
2. Hay, J R, *The Development of the British Welfare State*.
3. Calvert, I Mrs, *Northern Ireland House of Commons 1949, Welfare Services Bill*, (Second Reading).
4. Ibid.
5. *The Protection and Welfare of Young and the Treatment of the Young Offender*, (1946) Government White Paper. Cmnd 264, HMSO.
6. Ibid.
7. Ibid.
8. Evason, E, Darby, J, Pearson, M (1976), *Social Need and Social Provision in Northern Ireland*, NUU Coleraine.
9. Ibid.
10. Child Welfare Council (1954), *Interim Report on Juvenile Delinquency*, HMSO.
11. Child Welfare Council (1956), *Children in Care*, HMSO.
12. Personal communication from Mr T Shannon.
13. Jamison, E R (1968), 'Ye Olde Welfayre', *Contact Magazine*, Belfast Welfare Authority.
14. Brown, W D D (1968), 'Ye Olde Welfayre', *Contact Magazine*, Belfast Welfare Authority.
15. Annual Reports of the Ministry of Health and Local Government.
16. Child Welfare Council (1960), *The Operation of the Social Services in relation to Child Welfare*, HMSO.
17. Personal Communication from Miss M E Hall, former Principal Social Worker (Health Care), Eastern Health & Social Services Board.
18. Much of the above material is based on John Beresford's unpublished thesis (November 1976), *Some considerations on the Amalgamation or otherwise of the Northern Ireland Probation and After–Care Service into the Personal Social Services system in Northern Ireland*, NUU, Coleraine.
19. Child Welfare Council (1960), *Operation of the Juvenile Courts in Northern Ireland*, HMSO.
20. Child Welfare Council (1963), *Adoption of Children*, HMSO.
21. Child Welfare Council (1966), *The Role of the Voluntary Homes in the Child Care Service*, HMSO.
22. Child Welfare Council (1969), *Report on the Children and Young Persons Boarding-out Regulations*, HMSO.
23. Much of the material relating to training and staff development in the probation service is based on the notes of Mr Victor McElfatrick.
24. Gadd, Breidge (May 1975), 'Community Service Orders — a History of the Scheme', *Quest* – Journal No 3.
25. Darby, J & Williamson, A (eds) (1978), *Violence and the Social Services in Northern Ireland*, Heinemann.

Chapter III – Appendix
Summary of Relevant Legislation

1942	Children (Juvenile Courts) Act (NI)
1946	Public Health and Local Government (Administrative Provisions) Act (NI)
1948	Health Services Act (NI)
1948	Mental Health Act (NI)
1949	Welfare Services Act (NI)
1950	Children and Young Persons Act (NI)
1950	Adoption of Children Act (NI)
1950	Probation Act (NI)
1954	Welfare Services Act (NI)
1961	Welfare Services (Amendment) Act (NI)
1961	Mental Health Act (NI)
1967	Adoption Act (NI)
1968	Treatment of Offenders Act (NI)
1968	Children and Young Persons Act (NI)
1969	Adoption (Hague Convention) Act (NI)
1969	Health Services (Amendment) Act (NI)
1969	Community Relations Act (NI)
1970	Criminal Justice (Temporary Provisions) Act (NI)
1971	Payment for Debt (Emergency Provisions) Act (NI)
1972	Health and Personal Social Services Order (NI)
1973	Emergency Provisions Act (NI)
1976	The Treatment of Offenders (NI) Order
1978*	The Chronically Sick and Disabled Persons Act (NI)
1978**	Matrimonial Causes Order (NI)
1979	Matrimonial Causes Rules (NI)

* The main effect of this Act with regard to health and personal social services is to make certain functions mandatory which were already being performed by the Boards under the general powers of the Health and Personal Social Services Order (NI). For instance Boards are required to ensure that they are adequately informed of the numbers and needs of handicapped persons. (The 'Outset' survey helped to implement this function).

** This Order relates to matrimonial proceedings in the High Court. A judge may refer to a Board any matter concerning the welfare of a child, and a social worker may take on a reconciling or conciliating role. The Court may also make an order committing a child to care or a supervision order.

CHAPTER IV
'Personal' Social Services?

In his foreword to the Government pamphlet "Strategy for the Development of Health and Personal Social Services in Northern Ireland" (1975), Mr Roland Moyle made the following comments: "Everyone in Northern Ireland needs health care, whether at home or in hospital, at some stage of life, and very many also need social care. The health and personal social services are of vital importance to the whole community, and their maintenance and further advance are thus of prime concern to the Government.

The administration of these services was brought together in October 1973 under the four Health and Social Service Boards, each responsible in its area for providing integrated health and social care. The new administrative structure has now settled down, and gives opportunities as never before for planning and providing hospital and community services together in the best interests of the people who need them..." [1]

These fine sentiments must however be set alongside more objective statements about progress of the personal social services in identifying and meeting social needs. In spite of the management consultants' advice that the operation of the new structure should be monitored and adaptations made as necessary, only a half-hearted effort was made to do this. However sponsored by the Nuffield Provincial Hospitals Trust, the Department of Business Studies, Queen's University Belfast carried out two questionnaire studies administered by two research officers.[2] The first questionnaire survey was carried out six months after re-organization and it highlighted deficiencies even at this early stage:

> "There was very little certainty or confidence about objectives... Some of those interviewed confused objectives with functions, despite the fact that we had separated these two questions in the questionnaire. The lack of planning or implementation of programmes of care... may be one of the main reasons for this uncertainty about objectives."

> "Guidance from their superiors... appears to have been minimal and a few people suggested that this may be because their superiors were not sure of their own objectives and functions."

The research officers were charitable about these and other complaints (low morale, the two-tier area/district structure, the bureaucratic complexities) and regarded them as normal teething troubles of any new organization. The recurring criticism of the failure of programmes of care to develop is less easily answered.

The second report, completed two years after re-organization was less tolerant since many of the problems of the earlier report were found still to exist. The timing of the report, of course coincided with the beginning of inflation and the financial constraints which it brought. This camouflaged some of the underlying frustrations which were still there. Dissatisfying aspects mentioned include: lack of contact with staff on the ground; the increase in administrative and committee work; the lack of clear lines of responsibility; the cumbersome nature of the system. There were defects in communication: "lack of or delay in receiving budget information; lack of statistical information; lack of information from the Department of Health and Social Services; too much unnecessary or irrelevant information." "Little was known about the role of the Chief Administrative Medical Officer and District Administrative Medical Officer by other professions." "There was no programme of care in operation."

There were continuing criticisms of the two-tier district/area structure; "top heavy administration causing long delays in decision-making." "The Area Board has too little autonomy and is obliged to refer matters continually to the Department." "The structure encourages 'buck-passing' between the Department, area and district."

In its conclusion, the second report stepped outside its descriptive role and was critical of the indecent haste with which re-organization was introduced. The ploy about 'consultative documents' is exposed. "Consultation is only useful if it is also meaningful. It is meaningful only if those consulting are open to change in their proposals and those being consulted feel that their views may be incorporated in those proposals. It would appear that the initial proposal to have four Area Boards and the secondary proposal to have a two-tier system of administration were not open to change at that time."

> "We found little evidence in our interviews of involvement of even first-level district staff in planning though they supply much of the information to the planning teams. If a system is to be geared to the needs of the "consumer" then it follows that those closest to the "consumer" should be involved in planning services for them.
>
> "In conclusion, our impression of the development of the structure was that it developed working from the top down — making the districts fit the structure — rather than from an anlysis of need — developing a structure fitting the requirement of the districts, the areas and indeed the Province as a whole.
>
> "In both interview programmes we found uncertainty and frustration, even more in the second round than in the first round... The terms "low morale" and

'Personal' Social Services

"frustration" were used frequently in the second round of interviews. "There was clearly a high degree of uncertainty about the future."

Yet the grim realities of the present were soon to be spelt out in a study of social conditions in the Province. Eileen Evason in her study of the extent of poverty in Northern Ireland [3] stated that "Northern Ireland suffers from a unique combination of disadvantages, the effect of which is that families in this part of the UK are more likely to be in poverty than families in any other UK region". Her conclusions make salutary reading. In 1975, 30.4% of Northern Irish families had incomes below the needs level. These families contained 38.2% of all Northern Irish children (the needs level being the level of income at which families become entitlted to rent rebates from the Northern Ireland Housing Executive). Low wages, single parenthood and unemployment were identified as the three main causes of family poverty. (8.7% of families were identified as single parent families.) Children in Northern Ireland were concluded to be much more deprived than children in Britain as a whole. The study "Born to Fail" (Wedge and Prosser 1973) considered the proportion of British children handicapped by one or more forms of social disadvantage in 1969 — handicaps consisting of low income family; large family; one parent family; family subject to at least one form of housing stress. Evason compared these findings with an analysis of the 1975 Household Survey in Northern Ireland. The findings showed that in Northern Ireland the majority of children were socially disadvantaged in some way. In addition, about 14% of Northern Irish children suffered from all of the forms of social disadvantage described above compared with 6% in Britain.

The statistics relating to children in care which emerged from the Department of Health and Social Services Census of June 1977 reproduced in Table 25 also highlighted the importance of a more co-ordinated preventive programme of services for families.[4]

As can be seen from the Tables 25 and 26(over), three types of reason for admission to care predominated in all the Area Boards — neglect, a single parent unable to cope with problems, and no parent or guardian available to care for the child. It is also clear that religion continued to exert a central influence in determining residential placements. There was still in fact a marked trend towards using statutory homes for Protestant children and Catholic voluntary homes for Catholic children. There appeared to be at least two clear messages in these statistics. Firstly, supportive family casework services (as opposed to Civil Defence roles after flooding, rioting, etc) demanded recognition as an essential priority. Secondly, the question of adequate professional education and training for all residential social workers (statutory and

page 121

A Service for People

TABLE 25 : Main reason for children going into Care on 30 June 1977

Main reason for admission	Northern Ireland No	Northern Ireland %	Eastern Board %	Northern Board %	Southern Board %	Western Board %
1 Neglect	399	21.2	22.5	15.5	29.9	16.7
2 Single parent -unable to cope	376	20.0	15.8	26.6	17.2	26.4
3 No parent/guardian available	332	17.6	20.2	16.2	8.3	19.5
4 Long-term illness of caring parent	151	8.0	6.3	10.3	8.0	10.3
5 Child's behavourial problems	151	8.0	10.2	5.7	8.4	4.2
6 Non-accidental injury/physical assault	127	6.7	6.9	7.5	8.4	3.9
7 Family stress/ parental strife	66	3.5	3.6	1.0	3.4	6.4
8 Behavioural problems in caring parent	62	3.3	3.1	4.9	3.1	1.9
9 Rejection by parent(s)	53	2.8	4.1	1.5	0.8	2.3
10 Homeless	48	2.5	0.4	5.7	4.2	3.5
11 Short-term illness of caring parent	45	2.4	2.2	2.3	3.8	1.6
12 Prospective adoption breakdown of fostering	52	2.8	3.4	1.0	4.2	1.9
13 No relatives available	17	0.9	1.0	1.3	0	0.9
14 Not Known	4	0.2	–	–	–	–
Total	**1,883**	**100.0**	**100.0**	**100.0**	**100.0**	**100.0**

TABLE 26: Placement distribution according to time in Care

Time in Care	Statutory residential %	Voluntary residential %	Foster %	Home on trial %	Other %	No.
< 1 year	15.4	27.2	34.5	12.8	10.0	475
1-2 years	13.0	25.5	35.7	21.2	4.5	529
3-5 years	15.2	27.8	41.1	11.2	4.7	367
6-9 years	21.1	19.4	51.2	6.2	2.1	289
10 or more years	16.6	9.9	69.5	1.3	2.7	223

voluntary) needed to be vigorously pursued so that the emotional needs (as well as spiritual needs) of children in care could be properly met. While the overall percentage of children in care who were fostered was 42.9%, this reflected a wide variation throughout the Province. Certain areas in Belfast had a prominently low rate of boarding-out of children. It was indisputable that if professional standards in child care practice were even to be brought up again to the standards set in the late 1960s, then serious consideration had to be given to some form of specialist co-ordination and properly executed research and evaluation.

The Children and Young Persons Review Group (The Black Committee) which was established in 1976 eventually published its findings in December 1979. This long awaited Report produced recommendations which ranged from some which are laudably logical to others which were frustratingly ambivalent. The notion of a school-based care team made up of counsellors, education welfare officers, psychologists and social workers had much merit and would make for a more integrated approach to early identification of children in need of help. It was also timely that certain recommendations were made in terms of legislation. For instance there has been a statutory bias in our legislation in favour of boarding out children and the Black Committee wisely felt this should be removed. This was not to down-grade the strengths of fostering as a mode of dealing with a case — it was to leave decisions open to professional judgements in specific circumstances.

Similarly the Committee was on a sound footing when it suggests that the time was not ripe for the introduction of custodianship orders giving foster parents greater rights to the child in their care, as in the Children Act 1975 of England and Wales. Its conclusion that such provisions were as yet untried and that no case had been made for their use in Northern Ireland was perfectly tenable. The recommendation was also welcomed that a guardian ad litem be appointed to safeguard the child's interests in any case where there could be a conflict between the interests of the child and those of his parent or guardian.

It was also at first glance a constructive step to advocate the introduction of a "care order" into the legislation. This would enable the Boards through their professional social work staff, to decide the most appropriate form of care, be it residential care, boarding out or home supervision. As the Care Order made by the Court could remain in force until a child attained the age of eighteen, the Committee also recommended that there should be a court review of a care order at least every three years. This appeared to be a progressive move beyond the present system whereby children can be made subject to a Fit Person Order or a Training School Order with wildly varying assumptions and objectives underlying the decisions.

However it then transpired that the Black Committee advocated Care Orders only in care proceedings, and added that "it would not be possible for the juvenile court dealing with criminal cases to make a Care Order". The Committee then went on to state that, while "it is not possible to demonstrate conclusively that any age is particularly appropriate for knowledge of right and wrong", it did not wish to recommend any change in the age of criminal responsibility which at present stands at 10 years of age. It then proceeded to argue that "juvenile criminal courts" should be separate from courts dealing with care cases. For "more serious or persistent deliquents", the court would have the power to make a new custodial order which would replace the present Training School Order and Borstal sentence. The Order would have a minimum length of one month and maximum length of two years. A new custodial unit, catering for up to 120 boys and girls, with education and vocational training on the premises would be needed "to provide all the normal features of a humanitarian regime consistent with the need to exercise control over those committed to custody".

There were manifold dangers in such a scheme. It smacked of artificial and arbitrary distinctions between offenders and non-offenders. At worst it would reinforce a labelling process as the "juvenile criminal courts" selected out the children who were "clearly a threat to society". In setting out to extract principles derived from the "welfare" and "justice" models for dealing with juvenile offenders, the Black Committee had ended up with an impossibly ambivalent formula. It was advocating a split court structure which would deal with what it saw as at least three distinct types of organism — the child in need of care and protection; the delinquent going through a phase who is open to cautioning; the persistent delinquent who is a threat to society. While children's behaviour or visible circumstances can appear to fit such neat categories, the underlying causes are not always open to neat definitions — nor are the methods of coping with such difficulties as conveniently appropriate as the Black Committee suggests. It is to be hoped that any eventual changes in the constitution of the juvenile courts are made on the basis of more coherent and consistent arguments.

On the other hand, the conclusions of the Committee with regard to the probation service had compelling validity. It is important that the probation service remains a separate service continuing to develop its expertise in dealing with offenders and serving the criminal courts. The call for more involvement of the community in the management of the Service was welcomed by most probation officers. Instead of being administered directly by the Northern Ireland Office, the Black Committee recommended that the probation service be administered and managed by a Committee drawn from a wide spectrum of the community which would be empowered to appoint various sub-committees to look after different aspects of the work.

The Black Committee soundly decided to make Northern Irish adoption legislation the subject of a separate Consultative Document. Several recommendations emerged which strengthen the process of adoption considerably.

I It was proposed that independent placements of children for adoption with non-relatives, whether they are made by natural parents, relatives or strangers, should be prohibited. In other words, the best possible placement with non-relatives could only be made through the services of an adoption society.

II A "freeing order" was advocated, similar to that contained in the 1975 Children Act of England and Wales, through which parental rights could be transferred by the court to the adoption society. With proper safeguards built in, this could be a valuable way of removing the strain and anxiety on both the natural parents' and adoptive parents' part during the period of waiting before a final Adoption Order is made. The right of the adoption society to request a court to dispense with the parents' consent to a Freeing Order might well be a valuable step forward in the interest of many children who "wait" in care because of the uncertainty in relation to parental consent.

III It has been an anomalous situation in Northern Ireland that the Area Board involved in the placement of a child can also be appointed to act as guardian ad litem. The recommendation was timely therefore for the establishment of a panel of social workers from which persons could be selected to act as guardian ad litem or reporting officer (in the case of a Freeing Order application).

IV In line with the practices in Scotland, England and Wales, it was proposed that an adopted person on reaching the age of majority should not be denied access to his birth records. Counselling help might well be an important element in helping the adopted person reach a decision as to whether he should continue his investigations of his origins, but the principle was a sound one that an adopted person should have the right to claim this information on becoming an adult.

Another aspect of social work which needed to be given a sustained priority was the care of the elderly. Indeed there is a danger that we have less caring concern now for the elderly than our society did before the arrival of the statutory social services. The elderly cease to be useful in terms of productivity in our highly technical and industrialized world and they tend to be designated as a dependent burdensome class on their own. The present-day necessity for a skilled and concentrated social work service for the elderly was highlighted by Meryl Townsend's research in 1977, in which the population of Area Board Homes for the Elderly was analysed in detail.[5] It was noted that there were 2,500 elderly in Area Board Homes representing 15.4 per 1,000 females and 12 per 1,000 males in the general population.

A very significant finding was that 30% of all residents were over 85 years of age compared with 6% of the general population and within that 30% there were three times as many women as men. By applying a specially devised scale of social functioning, Townsend found that 33% of residents could be classified as "fit"; 20% were "less fit"; 33% were incapable of full self-care; 5% were "partly dependent"; and 18% were dependent (this category containing the most confused elderly). Certain tentative conclusions appear to arise from these findings. If one considers together the categories of "fit" and "dependent", then the question could be asked as to whether 51% of the residents were appropriately placed in the Area Board Homes. Another revealing finding was that only 4 people in the "fit" group were awaiting alternative housing and only 2 were in residential care for assessment purposes. The inescapable question that seems to require urgent attention was whether approximately 826 men and women could have been leading lives in their own houses, at least for a further period, had there been a more comprehensive social work service and pattern of facilities such as old people's dwellings and sheltered housing. Another issue raised by Townsend was whether Area Board Homes should be expected to cope with the intensity of care required by the "dependent" group, at least without a better staff-resident ratio. With the increasing proportion of very elderly dependent people in need of care, social work policy in Northern Ireland has the task of providing appropriate facilities which also provide a reasonable quality of life.

For instance, while some specialist segregated Homes had been established for the "confused" elderly in Northern Ireland, it was important to avoid the danger, under the glossy newness of a purpose-built establishment, of reverting to the old functions of Poor Law institutions in locking away the socially rejected from the public view.

Similarly the needs of the mentally and physically handicapped, the blind and the deaf needed to be protected. A census carried out in 1975 by the Northern Ireland Residential Social Work Liaison Group revealed that where qualifications existed at all in residential care for the groups mentioned above, these tended to be in the form of nursing qualifications.[6] Social workers and their administrative superiors have an essential responsibility to ensure that the socio-emotional implications of illness and handicap are not kept submerged by a medical model of practice which still dominates some of the more traditional institutions. Increased opportunities for the education and training of residential staff in general would hopefully contribute to positive changes in this respect.

The scope for improvement in professional practice was spelt out by a sub-committee of the Central Personal Social Services Advisory Committee in its report on Services for Hearing Impaired People (March 1977)[7]. It noted the paucity of statistical information available. Furthermore it was found that the last annual statistical return submitted to the Department of Health and Social Services based on the registers of handicapped persons held by Boards related to the year ended December 1973! The Sub-committee also made a plea for programme planning teams in each Board to develop a programme of care for the hearing impaired. In addition it called for a better liaison between Boards and voluntary bodies in the interests of extending the range of facilities for families. This did not appear to be solely a pragmatic argument to counter scarce resources but it carried a recognition that voluntary groups could foster self-help between deaf people themselves.

An opinion which came through strongly was that there should be increased opportunity for specialist work with the deaf in the Boards both in terms of post-qualifying training and the introduction of a specialist career structure to enable some staff to continue with their work and deepen their knowledge and skills. This recommendation reflected a lot of debate which was taking place at that time. On the one hand, the strong need was expressed generally for a social worker career grade which would have its reward in an enhancement of skills and a more insightful evaluation of the effectiveness of practice. Secondly there was a body of opinion that in many areas of practice, be it mental health, handicap, child care, there was a lack of depth of knowledge or even availability of sound consultation. It would appear that the generalist structure whereby most qualified social work staff were expected to carry a wide-ranging caseload and everyone above a team leader in the hierarchy was regarded as a "manager", was beginning to show its considerable limitations.

This was perhaps a further indication that the emphasis on professional social work courses themselves needed to be reviewed. Since the inception of the universal

A Service for People

"certificate of qualification in social work" for the British Isles, courses tended to operate on a "generic" basis, teaching students the common skills and knowledge applicable to a range of settings and only introducing them to more specialized areas of practice (whether it be in terms of techniques or client groups).

Northern Ireland now has four centres of professional social work training established at Queens University Belfast and two campuses of the University of Ulster at Jordanstown, and Magee College. The time was obviously ripe to collectively investigate the need for post-qualifying courses in areas of specialized interest and QUB led the way eventually with a post-qualifying course in Child Care.

It became clear from Government statements that the Northern Ireland probation service was to increase substantially its staffing, thus suggesting that the option of integration into the Area Boards had been put aside. Consequently Northern Ireland was still to have a service specifically committed to the needs of the offender and his family. While there was some weight in theory in the argument for a unified family service, it was probably beneficial to the Northern Irish community that the probation service consolidated its post-war growth as a separate entity. With its initiatives in areas such as Community Service Orders and intermediate treatment, it had developed a certain freshness and enthusiasm. There is no doubt that an all-embracing bureaucractic structure for personal social services could have had a very negative stultifying effect. Having said that, it was probably essential that the Northern Ireland probation service moved away from its inheritance of Civil Service domination and was given the opportunity to develop a Probation Committee system, enabling a much fuller participation of Court representatives in the on-going work of the service.

It was also imperative that the enthusiasm and expertise of the many voluntary organizations in Northern Ireland were not allowed to waste away through lack of support.

There is tremendous potential within many of the voluntary social work agencies whose origins pre-date the foundation of the statutory personal social services. The NSPCC, after a very rudimentary existence with perhaps in the past a rather judgemental prosecutory role towards families in distress, has had for some time a commitment towards social work training, both within its own training department in London and in the secondment of staff on to CQSW courses. Its Belfast office opened a student unit under the guidance and leadership of a professionally qualified social worker in the late 1970s. Of tremendous importance to social work generally, is the extensive pioneering work undertaken by the NSPCC into non-accidental injury to children and its experimental use of therapeutic pre-school playgroups and parent groups. Dr Barnardo's too has striven to develop a professional social work practice, moving a considerable way from the early paternalistic Christian zeal. Its exploratory work from the 1970s in the area of professional fostering was an indication of its important continuing role alongside statutory personal social services. The Down and Connor Family Welfare Society, with its professional social work team steadily improving the adoption placement practice and decision-making in relation to children in the care of voluntary Catholic Homes, was another example of the essential co-existence of statutory and voluntary social work. Likewise the Belfast Council of Social Welfare (formerly the Belfast Voluntary Welfare Society) continued to make an important contribution to beleaguered Belfast with its family casework service.

If future development of personal social services is to be imaginative and responsive to local needs, such organizations require encouragement and the sort of tangible support which would make them less dependent on public generosity on flag-days, while preserving their independent spirit. There have been indications in the past that while lip-service has been paid to the importance of voluntary work, only "well-behaved" voluntary groups will receive grant-aid. For example, central Government belatedly took the initiative in setting up the Northern Ireland Council on Alcohol in spite of the fact that two long-standing voluntary organizations were already in existence which shared similar aims: the Council on Alcohol-Related Problems (formerly the Irish Temperance League) and Alcoholics Anonymous.

The Wolfenden Report, "The future of Voluntary Organizations", made reference to Northern Ireland and the co-existence of established voluntary bodies and newly formed community groups. In a subsequent consultative document "Government and the Voluntary Sector", the possibility was indicated of a new independent grant-making Charitable Trust, and stressed its recognition of the importance of voluntary bodies in this region of "extensive poverty and social deprivation." [8]

In their useful study of voluntary organizations in Northern Ireland ("Yesterday's Heritage or Tomorrow's Resource"; NUU 1978), H. Griffiths, T. Ni Giolla Choille and J. Robinson concluded that there are two alternative models which characterize possible negative or positive perceptions of the future role of voluntary organizations. The "Heritage Model" assumes that most voluntary organizations are a throw-back to the nineteenth century, reflecting the efforts of the middle classes to assist those sections of the population less fortunate than themselves. Consequently in the face of expanding statutory health and social services they would be seen as increasingly irrelevant and what funds were made available would tend to be for high-risk ventures which coincide with the political needs of the Government. (In our view it would be an oversimplified distortion to apply such a model to the history of voluntary organizations in Northern Ireland). On the other hand, the "Resource Model" suggests that the relative decline of voluntary organizations after the introduction of the welfare state was only temporary and that the concepts of personal responsibility and expression

A Service for People

of collective responsibility for others are central to the development of personal social services. One vision cultivated by this model is of programmes of care to meet the needs of special groups delegated to the lowest practicable level, administered by local committees reflecting a wide range of representation. It is suggested that two groups which could be drawn into personal social services projects in the future under such a philosophy would be the retired and the unemployed.[9]

By 1980 there was a wide gulf between monolithic, bureaucratic structures remote from local communities with decision-making vested largely in central Government, acting through largely appointed Boards, and on the other hand individuals and community groups with no access to decision-making. That central Government was aware of the gulf was evidenced by the attempt to 'paper over the cracks' by means of projects like the Belfast Areas of Need Scheme (BAN) whereby central Government made money directly available for local projects, many of which should have been the responsibility of Health and Social Services Boards. This kind of cosmetic exercise was regarded as somehow replacing genuine local participation in determining local needs and priorities.

Even more obvious was central Government's failure to grasp the matter of genuine community development. Community work presupposes a readiness to encourage autonomy in local groups and to help them to articulate and meet local needs. The process can be a painful one since local communities are often critical of faceless civil servants. Having dismantled the Community Relations Commission which made a valuable start in the field, central Government diffused its energies to the four winds: some functions were farmed out to Education and Library Boards, particularly those with a youth component; others (mainly to do with leisure) went to the emasculated District Councils; the remainder, innocuous community service functions, were left to Health and Social Services Boards.

In summary, the following observations could be made about the first ten years after the re-structuring of Health and Social Services.

(a) Many of the concepts which the Management Consultants enunciated for the Area Boards were valid. These included 'programmes of care', 'programme planning teams' (as envisaged by them) and 'monitoring'. There was however no evidence that these had been taken seriously.

(b) Integration between Health and Social Services had not been shown to be viable. While there was some overlapping (in the care of the elderly, the disabled and the mentally disordered) there were many more aspects which they did not share (most of the child care field, delinquency, family casework).

(c) The personal social services failed to create a career structure which would promote professional social work development and this remained a priority if professional social work was to have a reasonable standing and credibility vis-à-vis other professions.

(d) There was a tremendous onus on social work education centres to provide courses that would help to promote more effective social work practice in Northern Ireland. In this connection positive discrimination was urged in favour of residential social workers' needs, as they had for too long been neglected second class citizens.

(e) Social services research needed to be very actively promoted. Expensive projects were still being embarked on (not least those of BAN) with no secure foundation in research.

(f) The place of professional community work needed to be re-appraised. Arrangements for participation by community groups were completely ineffectual.

(g) The important pioneering tradition of voluntary social work agencies should be preserved and safeguarded.

A Further Review of Board Structure & Management

Following the publication of the Report of the Royal Commission on the National Health Service in July 1979, a consultative Paper now addressed the specific proposals related to the structure, organization and management of the health and personal social services in Northern Ireland.[10]

In his foreword the Minister of State, Michael Alison, confirmed the recommendation of the Royal Commission that "the present integration of Health and Personal Social Services should be encouraged and further developed". He went on to assert that: "Independent research undertaken on the Commission's behalf suggests that this is also the view of most people involved in the provision of these services in Northern Ireland". Such a bland blanket statement contrasts vividly with the viewpoint of one senior manager in the personal social services who commented that: "Corporate management is like the Emperor's new clothes — it cost a lot of money to establish and its result have yet to be seen." In the light of the fact that the structures in Britain were to remain separate, there was an alarming lack of detailed evaluation of the effectiveness of the Health and Personal Social Services Board in Northern Ireland.

Indeed the general tenor of the Consultative Document reflected the preoccupation of the Commission: "to improve the quality and effectiveness of hospital administration and the status of the institutional manager." Hence one specific recommendation which

A Service for People

was put forward with great emphasis was that "below region in England, and elsewhere in the United Kingdom below health department, except in a minority of cases, one management level only should carry operational responsibility for services". It is then interesting to examine the criteria by which design of a structure below regional level in Northern Ireland was recommended. On the one hand, there was reference to areas being coherent in terms of "well-defined community identities". On the other hand catchment areas were defined as including the majority of the population who looked for services to an area's major hospital group. And consequently an area should not be too small for the planning and management of the range of acute medical services, community health and personal social services. It was also emphasized that the requirements of the major teaching hospitals must be a priority.

Three models were suggested for consideration of revised management arrangements:

(a) Districts within Boards would be retained but reduced in number and unit or sector management would be strengthened within them;

(b) Districts would be abolished and local management based on units or sectors composed of teams of medical staff, nurses, administrators and social workers. Day to day co-operation would replace the present District Executive Teams;

(c) Separate site management would be provided for the major teaching hospitals through a senior administrator and nursing officer working with medical staff and responsible directly to the Area Executive Team.

A sector team of administrator, nursing officer and social workers responsible solely for community care would work in parallel and also report directly to the Area Team.

A number of important implications arose from this Consultative Paper. The clear call for removal of a tier of management would lead to much more centralized decision-making. Even with a genuine spirit of delegation to local sectors or districts, this would almost inevitably lead to more and more central support services and even more complex channels of communication. And this would totally contradict the philosophy of the re-organization in 1973 which proclaimed the importance of de-centralization and wide delegation of authority to the lowest levels.

There was also a definite suggestion emerging that Districts, if not wholly abolished, should be reduced in number. This would mean that there would be fewer District Committees or indeed that they would be amalgamated into one forum for each Area. Evidence to date has indicated the need for greater accountability on the part of the professional staff to representatives of local needs, not less accountability. There seemed a distinct lack of safeguards to guarantee the extent of accountability and the quality of local representation.

What of the priorities for the personal social services themselves? Undoubtedly there were too many layers of middle management at District level. This has led to a situation where service goals have become more and more displaced by the voracious appetites of self-justifying administrative goals. Any new structure should be trying to ensure: greater delegation of responsibility and authority to local levels, including budgetary control; more responsiveness to feedback from social workers about priorities; proper research and evaluation of services; unambiguous acceptance of its accountability to the general public.

Clearly the Consultative Paper confirmed that the corporate Health and Social Services Boards would continue in some shape or form. The challenge remained to give them as human a face as possible.

CHAPTER IV
References

1. *Strategy for the Development of Health and Personal Social Services in Northern Ireland*, (1975) HMSO.
2. Department of Business Studies, Queen's University of Belfast. (First Report August 1974. Second Report April 1976), *The Reorganization of Health and Personal Social Services in Northern Ireland*, Sponsored by the Nuffield Provincial Hospitals Trust.
3. Evason, Eileen (1978), "Family Poverty in Northern Ireland," *Poverty Research Series No 6*, Child Poverty Action Group.
4. *Census of Children in Care* (June 1977), Department of Health and Social Services.
5. Townsend, Meryl (1977), *The Need for Care*, Social Work Advisory Group DHSS.
6. *Residential Staff Census* (November 1975), Northern Ireland Residential Social Work Liaison Group.
7. *Report on Services for Hearing Impaired People* (March 1977), Central Personal Social Services Advisory Committee.
8. *Government and the Voluntary Sector*, (1978) HMSO.
9. Griffiths H, Ni Giolla Choille T, Robinson J (1978), *Yesterday's Heritage or Tomorrow's Resource*, NUU.
10. *Consultative Paper on the Structure and Management of Health & Personal Social Services in Northern Ireland*, (December 1979) DHSS, HMSO.

CHAPTER V
The New Managerialism

In spite of the deficiencies we have outlined in the previous chapter, the new integrated structure did create some opportunities for development in the 1980s. While there had been earlier reviews of services for individual client-groups along 'programme of care' lines [1] the new sector arrangements facilitated a stocktaking of what was being provided for different groups of "persons in need".

Thus services for elderly people were comprehensively reviewed in a valuable report "Past 65, Who Cares?" [2] It clearly identified two priorities: the importance of developing dementia services for an increased proportion of elderly people and the need to maintain and expand domiciliary services.

The first of these recommendations has had some impact although more in the hospital than in the community sector. New 60-bed specialist psycho-geriatric hospital units have been opened in three psychiatric hospitals (Holywell in the Northern Board; Purdysburn in the Eastern Board and St Luke's in the Southern Board). Each of the six psychiatric hospitals now has a consultant psychiatrist with a special interest in the psychiatry of old age.

Residential and day-care services for people with dementia have fared less well. There are now 10 EMT (elderly mentally infirm) homes in Northern Ireland. Although standards vary between them they all provide a valuable specialist residential service and there is an increasing tendency for them to develop as resource centres to the local community. For example, in Ferrard House in the Northern Board people with dementia who are causing difficulties for families can come into the home for varying periods, partly to give the family a break, but also so that staff who have lived with the person for a time can offer constructive advice about problems. There are also flexible arrangements for follow-up in the person's own home by residential staff.

In day-care, it is still the case that there is no 7-day-a-week specialist day-centre service available although good, but limited, co-operative ventures between Boards and voluntary organizations exist. (Newington Day-Centre, a voluntary day-centre in North Belfast is a shining example.)

Domiciliary services have suffered most from the recent financial constraints imposed on Boards. The origins of the home help service have been sketched-in in Chapter III. It has differed from Home Care Services in England in having been largely

page 135

A Service for People

a 'casual', neighbourhood-based service. Statistics suggest that elderly people — the main recipients of the service — receive three times more Home Help hours than in England. It could be argued that this reflects elderly people's preferences and stated Government policy to maintain people in their own homes. Instead of consolidating this Service, it is one of the first to suffer in times of financial stringency.

Because home helps in the past have been a casual work-force, they are seen as an easy target for hard-pressed community units of management to effect savings quickly. This has been done in several ways: by means of a blanket percentage reduction with no regard to individual need or by imposing limits on the duties home helps can perform, for example eliminating cleaning. This again disregards need and the potentially preventive nature of a cleaning service in maintaining morale among elderly people who may be having increasing difficulty in coping with housework.

There have also been negative side-effects as a result of the move away from a casual, neighbourly service towards a whole-time workforce with full terms and conditions. The effect in one unit of management has been to discontinue providing home helps at week-ends because enhanced payments for week-end working add to the wage-bill.

Ironically, running alongside a service which is increasingly under threat, is another Government Department's job-creation scheme which has substantial funds but no clear policy about how to use them — the Department of Economic Development ACE Scheme (Action for Community Employment — the English equivalent is the Department of Manpower Services Scheme). This has been spawning numerous community-based initiatives, often in competition with statutory community care services but with no structured co-ordination.

Turning to physical and sensory disability, unlike the other client groups, there has been no review of services even though there have been two major pieces of legislation: the Chronically Sick and Disabled Persons Act 1978 and the Disabled Persons Act 1990. Significantly these were both Private Members' Bills, suggesting a degree of reluctance on the Government's part to promote them, a point confirmed by the fact that they are being implemented in a piecemeal fashion. Both Acts in Northern Ireland, of course, mirror the English legislation.

The Chronically Sick & Disabled Persons Act imposes a duty on Boards to "inform themselves of the number of people who are substantially handicapped by illness, injury or congenital deformity and whose handicap is of a permanent or lasting nature" — to provide services, including

    practical assistance in the home,
    access to recreational facilities,

transport,
housing adaptations to improve safety, comfort or convenience,
telephones.

The Disabled Persons Act (only parts of which have to date been implemented in Northern Ireland) requires Boards to carry out an assessment of the needs of disabled school leavers; imposes a duty on Boards to take into account carers' ability to continue to provide care; requires the co-option to committees of people representing the interests of disabled persons.

It is a noteworthy deviation from the usual principle of parity between English and Northern Irish legislation that, in England, the opportunity was taken to incorporate parts of the Disabled Persons Act 1986 into the National Health Service and Community Care Act 1990 whereas the broadly similar health & personal social services Order 1991 is solely concerned with the administrative arrangements surrounding the health and social services reforms which are described in Chapter VI. Physically and sensorily disabled people are among the most vocal in rightly demanding to be able to lead a normal life. It would have been an acknowledgement of these rights to have entitlement enshrined in legislation, as is the case in England.

As occurred with services for elderly people, services for mentally ill people were reviewed in a document entitled "The Way Forward."[3] This is an inferior report which does not have the breadth of vision of "Past 65. Who Cares?" It fails to address the issue of large numbers of people still being accommodated in Victorian asylum buildings, the majority of whom are voluntary patients with nowhere else to go.

The inappropriately titled "The Way Forward" is still heavily hospital-dominated and failed to foresee the significant part which mental health voluntary organizations were to play in developments in the 1980s, although it did acknowledge the important work being carried out by the Industrial Therapy Organization (ITO). The report even suggested that ITO should be responsible for all mental health day-care, a proposal which under-estimated the degree of bureaucratic control exercised by Boards, quite apart from the interests of other voluntary organizations.

In residential care, the 1980s saw the closure of a number of mental health facilities, apparently due to lack of demand. But more accurately this reflected disagreement; on the one hand with consultant psychiatrists who equated community care with 24-hour nursing supervision under their control and, on the other hand, social services departments which now lacked the professional expertise of the former cadre of (mostly hospital-based) psychiatric social workers and who therefore lacked confidence in offering what was a potentially expensive service.

As in dementia services, it is still true in 1991 that specialist statutory mental health day centre provision is absent, with one or two exceptions (for example Melrose Day-Centre in Londonderry).

The picture is strikingly different in **mental handicap Services**.[a] Here too services were reviewed in 1978.[4] Prior to 1973, mental handicap had been the responsibility of the Northern Ireland Hospitals Authority (working through a sub-group known as the Special Care Authority) and as a result was largely hospital-based. To parents this had the virtue of simplicity and continuity since one organization had responsibility for mentally handicapped people "from the cradle to the grave". However, the system also had the unfortunate effect of segregating mentally handicapped people from the rest of society, both in regarding hospital as appropriate "residential" care and in having segregated education in "Special Care" schools.

Restructuring in 1973 meant a greater potential for social services involvement and the period from that date to 1990 has seen major community developments in the form of the integration of mentally handicapped children into ordinary education, a significant expansion of small, community-based hostels, an increase in special needs housing through housing associations and substantial investment in social education centres (although it has been recognized rather late in the day that 150-place centres can themselves be segregationist and non-normalizing).

Given this success story with an almost complete transformation from a hospital-based to a social services-led community service, it is difficult to see why a similar movement away from institutional care has been inhibited in the elderly care and mental health fields.

The Kincora Boys' Hostel Scandal

A "scandal" is defined by the Oxford Dictionary as "a thing that occasions general feelings of outrage or indignation especially as expressed in common talk or opprobrium". Ultimately the much over-used word was attached appropriately to the discovery that boys in a statutory residential hostel in Belfast had been subjected to sexual abuse by members of staff over a long number of years. However, when the details of the extent of this abuse and the nature of the responses to earlier allegations were made public, it became evident that the professional administrators responsible for child protection refused to believe that their residential care workers would be capable of such deeds in relation to their vulnerable young charges.

---

[a] For a comprehensive review of the development of mental handicap services in Northern Ireland see J S Fitzpatrick's MSSc thesis "Mental Handicap" 1989.

In a sense, the Kincora case was symbolic of the state of awareness in the wider societies in Britain and Ireland. Physical abuse of youngsters had long since been recognized as an aberration among some parents of all social classes and research had begun to identify the features associated with battered child syndromes. Apparent contradictions such as children from relatively well-off families with fastidious parents being subjected to uncontrolled and savage abuse were now being analysed and helping strategies were being worked out based on new insights. But in Northern Ireland in 1980 it was inconceivable that salaried staff in the employ of the welfare authorities would take such grotesque advantage of youngsters who had been placed in their care usually because of family breakdown.

In January 1980, the first publicly documented statement about Kincora appeared in the *Irish Independent*, containing information provided by two concerned social workers. In this article, it was asserted that boys as young as twelve years old were being sexually abused by male staff, that one boy had actually committed suicide as a direct result of being abused, and that homosexual prostitution was being promoted which had links with local businessmen and paramilitary groups. By December 1980, three staff from Kincora and three other men had been convicted and sentenced in the courts. The offences, forty nine in number, consisted of buggery, indecent assault and gross indecency.

It also transpired that as far back as 1967 two residents had forwarded written complaints to the then Belfast Welfare Authority alleging that their Warden was abusing them. These allegations appear to have been dismissed as malicious and, although the warden (one of the people to be convicted later) was interviewed, no further action was taken. Subsequently over a period of thirteen years, there had been repeated complaints and allegations to administrators and the police, but all had been disregarded as either malevolent or unsubstantiated.

Something of a tragi-comedy of errors then took place over a two year period. The Royal Ulster Constabulary reassured the public that it was actively investigating the wider allegations of a network of involvement. A Committee of Enquiry established by the Secretary of State in January 1982 was wound up in disarray because three members, including an English social work professor, resigned on the grounds that police investigations were still continuing.

Constructively, in the interim, the DHSS appointed a team to advise the Northern Irish social services administrators on the wider issues of supervision and management of homes and hostel for children and young persons. Chaired by A M Sheridan, the Report was published in December 1982 and contained sensible recommendations concerning the need for : a formal and comprehensible complaints procedure; effective monitoring of all residential establishments by professional officers; and training opportunities for residential staf. [5] These were broad practical recommendations that took approximately two weeks to formulate!

Parallel to this the Terry Report to the Director of Public Prosecutions in October 1982 had declared that there was no evidence of any vice network and that no criminal proceedings or disciplinary measures within the RUC were being recommended.

It was only in 1984 that the Government, under pressure to bring the full facts into public view, appointed a committee under the chairmanship of Judge William Hughes which would be "public" but would report to the DHSS. Working to a wide brief concerning the Committee's terms of reference included:

— inquiry into the administration of all Homes and Hostels whose young residents had been subjected to sexual abuse leading to court convictions (in cases other than Kincora these offences had taken place outside the Home and staff were not involved);

— investigation of practices concerning supervision and protection of the children;

— recommendations as to ways of promoting the welfare of the children. (Hughes Report 1984.) [6]

In all, the Committee received evidence from 185 former residents of Homes and Hostels. There were nine residential Homes involved, including one under the auspices of the De la Salle religious order, and two Dr Barnardo's homes. Further allegations of a network conspiracy from Colin Wallace, a former member of British Intelligence, and Valerie Shaw, a free Presbyterian missionary, were not followed up as they were deemed to be outside the terms of reference of the inquiry.

Kelly and Pinkerton argue that the Hughes Report represented itself as "the final and full account of the Kincora affair, thus turning the Kincora affair into a residential social work child care practice and management affair".[7]

Of the 56 recommendations, a substantial number referred to management procedures in relation to monitoring and control, and only seven tackled specific issues to do with child care practice. In effect, all the staff of residential childcare were made the scapegoats with an emphasis in future practice placed on "safety first". Kelly and Pinkerton assert that inevitably this detached view of childcare practice would lead to a growing detachment from children, erosion of confidentiality because of the pressure to report all incidents, and a repression of sexual matters instead of a healthy and open debate. They also maintained that this tendency to stifle further discussion on the wider implications of Kincora was reflected in the political response of the Government, which appeared to write Kincora off as an historical aberration, a one-off to be cast back into the Dark Ages and forgotten about.

In a tour de force of a paper at the North-South Child Welfare Conference in 1986, Jim Lynch elaborated on the dangers of this form of denial of reality:

"The secret is returned to oblivion from whence it came. Through the medium of investigation, interrogation and pseudo-publication, the powers that be in this society return the hidden truth to its owners, return it to their care; and of course the story begins all over again" (Lynch 1986 pps 16/17). [8]

Citing three examples in the Republic of Ireland, Lynch went on to assert that the apparent collusion between the agents of the State to compartmentalize child abuse as confined to a few deviants was not a phenomenon confined to the North:

"The Northern attenders at the first of our conferences (1985) foretold that the Kincora phenomenon would spread to the South. They were wrong. It had, as I have discovered since then, already become rampant within it." (Lynch 1986 p 24) [9].

So the Kincora "scandal" proved to be a short-lived affair. It took four years after the first newspaper article to set up a committee of inquiry and the findings of that committee were rationalized as putting a seal on the past by politicians and policy-makers. This seemed to placate and reassure not only the professional administrators in the social services but the public at large. It was really deemed to be the isolated and unique manifestation of deviant individuals' unnatural leanings towards children. The population could read the accounts, gasp in shock and express opprobium. But nothing ensued in official publications which encouraged a wider and more profound reflection on its significance in terms of human relations. The statutory services acted in lieu of the family in relation to deprived youngsters; the solution to the abuse of this role was to recommend even more rigid forms of social control. Totally disregarded was the impact on residential workers who were frozen into a defensive state, confused and ambivalent about the appropriateness of their human relations with the children in their charge. Sad to relate, it is likely that the very children in our society who would benefit greatly from expressions of love and concern, both verbal and tactile, are suffering the effects of a more cautious social distance encouraged and imposed on their carers as a fabricated preventative measure. In reality, the substitute world of residential child care has indeed been scapegoated and the guardians of statutory welfare have failed to explore honestly the complex and at times ambivalent and discomfiting depths of human relationships.

This continuing trend towards centralized control is illustrated by 'Community Care' in a recent investigation into the Area board management structures. [10] Because of the fact that Directors of social services have been removed from direct line management, childcare issues are the responsibility of the newly styled unit general managers and childcare managers, neither of whom need know anything about professional social work practice. In the same article L Boyle, Chairman of the British Association of social workers (N Ireland Branch) comments that:

> "Even at first line management level, or team leader, professional management could be overshadowed by general management" (op cit p. 13 1991). [11]

Not only in relation to child care but in the general provision of social services, there is a continuing replacement of a critical and reflective approach to professional practice by a diffuse and fragmented collectivity of "managers". Their role appears to be the maintenance of social stability through bureaucratic control.

Step by Step Adoption Legislation

Replicating the 1975 Adoption Act for England and Wales, the Adoption (NI) Order of 1987 was eventually implemented in 1989. It makes the provision of adoption agencies a mandatory duty of the social services Boards. Of central significance was the realization of the right of adopted children on reaching eighteen years to have access to the records of their natural parents. However anyone adopted prior to the legislation is required to undergo counselling as a condition of being given access to these records. While the report of the guardian ad litem is required for all agency and family placements, the Order did not make this GAL role totally independent of the agencies, with the result that one Area Board can still be the placement agency and provide the guardian ad litem report. In practice, the Boards try to ensure that the GAL is not an officer from the same placement district.

The Proposed Children Order

A draft Order is expected to be published in early 1992. Professional lobbyists hope that their arguments for an independent panel of Child Advocates will be implemented in this Order, given the vulnerability of children when there is a conflict of interests with parents or indeed professional agencies. It is widely expected that this new Order will combine the philosophy of involvement of parents and respect for their rights with an emphasis on child protection measure. Care Orders will be introduced and "Place of Safety" Orders will be replaced by shorter "Emergency Protection" Orders. However welfare and justice issues will be kept separate so there will be no quantum leap towards a Scottish Panel or a Family Court. In practice it seems likely that "family proceedings" will be heard in the same physical location of the Magistrates Courts as juvenile justice cases but on separate days. Resident magistrates and their lay assistants will remain as the arbiters. Area Board social workers will be able to place children in Training

Schools in the "care" sections, but in the interim it would seem that Training School Orders will remain. Hence the nettle of an archaic institution system for juvenile offenders will not be scrapped although, in reality, it seems likely that the Training Schools will gradually lose their traditional identity.

"Working for Patients" or *People* First"

During the 1980s the Conservative Government carried out a systematic review of most aspects of social policy: social security, housing, education, health and social services. There were several key themes common to these policy reviews: efficiency, value for money, delegation of decision-making to the lowest feasible level, choice for the consumer and the encouragement of private enterprise.

In social services, certain other developments coincided with and contributed to the need to review how services were being provided.

Firstly, social security reforms had introduced income support and, within it, the Social Fund. New income support arrangements meant that people entitled to income support wishing to enter private and voluntary residential and nursing home care could have the cost met up to a ceiling figure which is revised annually. While this increased choice for potential residents it also fairly predictably led to a large increase in the provision of private residential and, more particularly, nursing home care. (The income support differentials between residential homes and nursing homes have recently widened further in favour of nursing homes thus strengthening this more institutional end of the market.) These new moves were clearly contrary to Government policy reiterated over a number of years of planning to meet people's expressed wish to remain in their own homes while this was humanly possible.

Furthermore, this was only one aspect of the chaos within community care services of which the influential Audit Commission Report "Making a Reality of Community Care", published in 1986, was critical. It pointed to the maze of provision which people had to find their way through; the lack of co-ordination and clear responsibilities and the need for identified key-workers to help people with information, advice and, if necessary, advocacy. In addition, there was a movement which was gaining momentum for the consumer's voice to be heard. This was probably most evident in the case of mental handicap but it is also articulated in the Disabled Persons Act 1986. Finally, but not least importantly, there was a similar movement among carers, who increasingly sought acknowledgement for the fundamental part they play in community care.

These kinds of issues led the Government to commission Roy Griffiths (subsequently Sir Roy Griffiths) to review community care and to make recommendations

A Service for People

for change. He had, of course, been similarly commissioned to undertake a management inquiry into the National Health Service some years previously which had led to the introduction of General Managers. His findings and recommendations for community care were not dissimilar to his NHS review. In a businesslike approach he differentiated between social care and the more expensive health care, making the fairly obvious value for money point that it was important that people should not be consuming expensive health care unnecessarily. Although this is an important distinction, it has since been blurred, not least in Northern Ireland. He accepted the many criticisms of the Audit Commission Report, including the "perverse incentive" of open-ended social security entitlements for residential and nursing home care. In particular he emphasized the importance of a single authority having clear responsibility and since community care largely meant social care, social services departments were an appropriate choice.

While he was not asked to comment on resources, he did underline the importance of adequate resources and that these should be 'ring-fenced'. The report also recommends clearly designated key workers, whom he somewhat confusingly referred to as "care managers". (Confusion between 'key workers', 'case managers'[12] and 'care managers' has been one of the hallmarks of the new community care policy.)

Maximum delegation, together with a delegated budget, is another theme. While most of Griffiths' recommendations were accepted in principle (the designation of a "Minister for Community Care" and the proposal to 'ring-fence' budgets were not accepted) they have gone through certain transformations and delays. They did, however, lead to the publication of the Government's White Paper "Caring for People" 1989[13] and contributed to the National Health Service and Community Care Act 1990.

What significance did these changes have for Northern Ireland? They were a source of embarrassment both in timing and substance. In England, the Community Care reforms had been pre-dated by almost a year by the NHS White Paper "Working for Patients" 1989. This introduced a new delegation away from Regions to District Health Authorities, to individual hospitals and the proposed new self-governing trusts. Fundamental to the new arrangements is a clear distinction between the Region as determiner of the health care needs of its resident population and as purchaser of services to meet these needs. Purchasing is controlled by a system of service agreements or contracts. Districts, hospitals and trusts are in the business of providing services in accordance with these agreements. It is hoped that, by introducing an element of competition, efficiency will be improved and patients will have greater choice. The introduction of capital charging means that hospitals are no longer "free": their capital value needs to be taken into account.

"Caring for People" has separate chapters about arrangements in Wales and Scotland, but because of the integrated service in Northern Ireland it was decided to have a free-standing policy paper "People First"[14] which repeated much of the content of "Caring for People" but inevitably fudged some issues. However, there was a delay in issuing "People First"[14] with the result that NHS-type reforms were already in place. In other words, the community care reforms had to be made to fit in with Health Service arrangements. The two sets of administrative arrangements simply did not match. The effect of the Health Service reforms has been to strengthen general management at area level and to introduce it at Unit of Management level. For a population of 1.5 million this means that there are some 26 general managers.

Units of management can be single hospitals, groups of hospitals, community units, community plus hospital units or, in two instances, "area-wide mental health units of management." The last-named have the significant disadvantage of blurring the distinction between 'area' as planner and 'unit' as provider, quite apart from the effect of divorcing mental health services (unlike mental handicap services) from the communities they serve.

General management at area level have felt the need for reinforcement and consequently one has a raft of assistant area general managers. For example, the Eastern Board has a Director of Planning, a Director of Operations, a Director of Finance, a Director of Human Resources, a Director of Estate in addition to a Director of Public Health, a Director of social services and a Director of Nursing. Inevitably units of management have felt the need to mirror these arrangements at unit level. The result has been even greater confusion, over-manning and delays in making decisions. If one adds to this that each Unit of Management has different designations for essentially similar posts, the potential for bewilderment among recipients of the services is apparent.

Once this elaborate bureaucratic structure was in place, attempts had to be made to graft community care services on to it and this simply cannot work. The split between area as planner/purchaser and units/hospitals/trusts as providers makes sense where providers are large units like hospitals, but in community units where services are based in local communities and where voluntary organizations, carers and other self-help groups are likely to be providers, communications become more complex and confused, not least from the consumer's point of view. Voluntary organizations are increasingly unclear about whether they will be contracting directly with area, directly with units, or indirectly with area (ie sub-contracting with units). The situation is least clear in the two "area-wide mental health units" where detailed, prescriptive 'shadow' contracts are being drawn up which are likely to undermine good working relationships.

As serious, and in sharp contrast to England, professional authority has been significantly eroded in the context of general management. The role of Director of

Public Health is retained (and is incorporated in legislation) but it is a purely advisory role and does not carry any executive authority. Unlike England, where social services departments are clearly identified as the lead department, Directors of social services no longer have any status, legal or otherwise and social services cannot be singled out from the integrated structure since they have no separate identity in the setting of general management.

The effect of these reforms on social work and social services has been disastrous. Senior staff with substantial experience of managing social services have left the service. Younger, well-trained and experienced social workers have been sidetracked into quasi-managerial positions for which they are ill-equipped; professional advice at area level is seen as a dead-end in career development terms. Again, unlike England, social workers are by no means regarded as an automatic choice as case managers even though case-management skills are an essential component of traditional social work training. The effect on services has been, at best, ambiguous.

The new structure does offer opportunities to plan and deliver a comprehensive and integrated programme of care for each of the client-groups. However, since this was one of the foundations for the 1973 restructuring and failed to materialize it is difficult to be optimistic about the 1990 reforms being more successful. Early indications are that it is more likely in units of management where hospitals are an integral part of total provision. In practice, this applies to two units only: Down and Lisburn, and Bannside.

As an example of the fragmentation which can still occur one can refer to mental health services in Newtownards, which is in the North Down and Ards Units of Management. There are two psychiatric facilities in Newtownards: a small acute in-patient unit and a 30-place psychiatric day-hospital. The four consultant psychiatrists who work in these facilities also have long-stay beds in Downshire Hospital (which is in Downpatrick and is managed by Down and Lisburn Unit of Management). In other words, in the case of Newtownards the facilities are **geographically** in North Down and Ards Unit of Management; **professionally** in part at least, in Down and Lisburn Unit of Management and **managerially** in the Ulster and North Down and Ards Hospitals Unit of Management.

Services for elderly people.

In the late 1980s and early 1990s one of the most striking features of services for elderly people has been the immense growth in private nursing homes. This mirrors the position in England but for some reason, the private sector was slower off the mark in Northern Ireland. It is now rapidly catching up.

This growth — almost certainly the result of the new social security arrangements coupled with, in the early stages, the availability of capital grant from the local Enterprise Development Unit — is particularly anomalous in Northern Ireland where the number of hospital beds per capita is higher than in England. Two other sources of concern are the imbalance between nursing homes, as compared with residential home provision and the increasing size of individual nursing homes (in some instances over 80 beds). The result is 'transinstitutionalisation' in the community — the transfer of people from one institution to another. It is ironic that one of the largest statutory old people's homes in Northern Ireland — Ben Madigan in the Northern Board with 94 places — was planned to close, partly because its size was inappropriate. Instead it has been bought by a private concern and is now a nursing home. This large increase in private residential and nursing homes places has had an effect on the demand for statutory old people's homes. The opportunity has been taken to offer enhanced respite care facilities, to pioneer innovative hospital after-care schemes and, in a number of homes, to adapt parts of the home for use by elderly people with dementia.

The risk of over-provision is also present in the field of sheltered housing for elderly people. Here, too, there has been substantial expansion during the 1980s but no agreement between the Department of the Environment and the Department of Health and social services about an appropriate scale of provision. A jointly-funded research project carried out by the Policy Research Institute suggested that saturation point was being reached but its findings have been ignored.

If Government policy of maintaining people in their own homes for as long as possible is to be taken seriously one could expect an expansion in day-care and, to an even greater extent, domiciliary care. This has not happened. The failure to develop an adequate dementia day-care service has already been mentioned in Chapter V as has the continuing vulnerability of the home help service. Fortunately, voluntary organizations continue to show the way in seeking to meet individual need as will be described below.

Disabled People.

A similar comment applies to services for disabled people. There have been positive developments on the social security front as regards disability premiums. Statutory social services developments have been negligible although there have been some improvements in community-based occupational therapy staffing. Their role relationships within social services are not clear as in England, since ultimately they are professionally accountable on the medical side. There have also been improvements in the number of mobility and technical officers for blind people and enhanced training opportunities for training in communication with hearing-impaired people. However, the main innovative projects have again been by the voluntary sector.

Mental Handicap.

Statutory services have continued vigorous efforts to meet the needs of families through the development of special needs units for multiply handicapped adults in social educational centres. The Southern Health and Social Services Board took the lead in establishing family placement schemes for children and adults and these have now been taken up by other Boards. The imaginative recruitment methods and information leaflets produced make one wonder why social services in Northern Ireland are not credited with the ability to assume responsibility for other client groups.

Mental Illness.

The 1986 Mental Health Order (Northern Ireland) introduced specialist training for approved social workers. (This part of the Order was not implemented until 1988.) Boards and universities have co-operated well in providing good quality training (validated by the Central Council for Education and Training in Social Work). There is no doubt that the standard of social work in the fields of mental health and mental handicap has benefited.

In service provision, there has been a failure to grasp the nettle of the future of the six large psychiatric hospitals in Northern Ireland. The Donaldson Report[15] made the reasonable recommendation that each Board should be self-sufficient in its psychiatric services. (Prior to 1983 Holywell Hospital in Antrim served the Northern Board and parts of the Eastern Board; Downshire Hospital in Downpatrick served the Eastern Board and part of the Southern Board; Gransha Hospital in Londonderry served the Western and Northern Board, while Tyrone and Fermanagh Hospital served the Western, Northern **and** Southern Boards). But even so there are no firm plans to close any of the six hospitals. It is sometimes suggested that this is because Northern Ireland has learned the lessons of premature hospital closures in England. Such a specious argument does not address the issue of why an allegedly integrated service had such difficulty in shifting the balance of care from hospital to the community.

Nevertheless, the Eastern Board, for example, used bridging funds constructively to improve staffing levels in mental health hostels and the two Belfast Community Units of Management have developed a comprehensive residential and day-care service.

The Voluntary Sector.

Several references have been made to the crucial contribution which voluntary organizations have made either in pioneering new services; in substituting for statutory services or in partnership with the statutory sector. This has been particularly important at a time when statutory services often seemed paralyzed into inaction due to restructuring.

In services for **elderly people** the significant contribution of the voluntary Housing Association movement has already been mentioned. The Crossroads Care Attendant scheme — spanning several client-groups — has demonstrated how to provide flexible care in the person's own home using local management committees but with sound central support. Other specialist schemes, such as intensive home care after discharge from hospital[16] and tailor-made services for carers of relatives with dementia[17] have also broken new ground.

In the case of **younger disabled people**, Habinteg Housing Association has made a reality of the concept of full integration of disabled people in ordinary housing, while the Cheshire Foundation schemes in Belfast and Londonderry facilitate maximum support in a normal environment.

Voluntary services in **mental handicap** have been less numerous but there are imaginative projects bridging the gap between the relatively sheltered environment of social education centres and the real world of open employment.

However the most exciting revelation has been the growth of the voluntary sector in **mental health**, the area where arguably there has been the greatest inertia in the statutory sector.

The Northern Ireland Association for Mental Health has developed steadily and now offers 17 small group homes supported by local house committees; Beacon House clubs in all parts of the Province; an increasing number of mental health resource centres, at least one of which (in Ballymena) has a formal psychiatric out-patient session two days a week. The Association involves many volunteers and both through them and through its information services projects a posititive image of mental health. The Association is also pioneering a Patients' Council in Holywell Hospital and a Framework project (involving users in the planning of mental health services) in partnership with the Southern Health and social services Board.

The Industrial Therapy Organization which operated for many years in Downpatrick has now expanded, with the assistance of generous European Community funding and has opened factories in Newry, Bangor and Antrim with a fourth innovative project shortly to open in Enniskillen in the Western Board.

Praxis has established its befriending scheme in several centres and is now developing into the fields of Dispersed Intensive Support Housing and staffed hostels.

The National Schizophrenia Fellowship has drop-in centres for people with schizophrenia (whose day-care needs are significantly different) in Belfast, Newry and Lurgan. Its Haven project in Newcastle, County Down provides respite care, while longer-term special needs housing for young people with schizophrenia is offered at Fortwilliam in North Belfast. The Fellowship has strong user representation through its Voices scheme.

The Richmond Fellowship, a relative newcomer to Northern Ireland, has already opened two well-staffed hostels for older people with schizophrenia and a hostel for adolescents in South Belfast. A further hostel will shortly open in Armagh, and Kinahalla, outside Newry, will be an innovative residential outward bound centre for young people who have been through the Training School system (Community Homes with education in England). These facilities are provided with the Richmond Fellowship's well-known high standards of professional training, support and supervision.

Limited Legal Change

The most significant legislation affecting the probation service in the 1980s was the Probation Board Order of 1982. As a result the service ceased to be an integral part of the Northern Ireland Office and became part of a public body managed by an appointed Board. While the structural accountability changed profoundly, the actual statutory functions of the probation officers remained as before. Six years on from the British Criminal Justice Act of 1983, a Treatment of Offenders (NI) Order (1989) introduced a Fourth Condition on to the existing Probation Order. In practice this meant that the subject could be required either to attend a day centre or participate in a specified programme of activities up to a maximum of sixty days. So the Northern Irish service now could seek the Court's consent to various forms of intensive community supervision, which could include serious offenders.

However this legislation did not really help the Service to progress beyond the practice in which it had been engaged since the 1970s. Arguably the Northern Ireland Office, after the introduction of Direct Rule, had been so preoccupied by the security issues in the North that the ordinary criminal justice policy had been given a secondary priority. An instance of this is the fact that the recommendations on the Black Committee were not comprehensively followed up. In fact the only tangible development in the 1980s relating to juvenile justice was the joint DHSS/NIO statement in 1986 that the Black proposals had been re-considered and that the Training Schools were to remain in existence. It could be that this decision, no doubt influenced by the effective lobbying of Training School managements, delayed rather than prevented their eventual demise. Be that as it may, other opportunities were also spurned to develop a clear policy of diversion of juveniles from Courts, and of integrating preventive work properly within the probation and social services systems.

Judging from recent announcements, the DHSS is now preparing a new Children's Act but juvenile offending is not going to be incorporated within this legislation. It appears that the NIO is going to produce an Order in Council, not a substantive Act, but a collation of loose legal ends. Unfortunately this will do little to reinforce the good practice which already exists in the probation service. However this is sporadic and depends on the goodwill of a progressive magistrate. The negative side of the same coin, because of the retarded nature of the legislation, is that some Courts may send a juvenile to Training School on the basis of the same offence and similar record, who might be given an absolute discharge in another Court.

The Structure of the Service

Structurally, however, the probation service with its new relative autonomy has also been developing an ethos of its own. Members of the governing Board are appointed by the Secretary of State for a three year term (maximum six years service), and are theoretically drawn from a wide cross-section of the community. The Board in effect is charged with the responsibility of ensuring the effective delivery of the probation service, and is allocated an annual budget by the NIO. Because of the tight financial control exercised by the NIO, it would appear that the "independent" existence of the Service is sometimes more an appearance than a reality: for instance the Probation Board cannot spend any sum over £3,000 without NIO approval. While accountability for public spending is of course imperative, this does appear very limiting vis-à-vis a vibrant energetic service wanting to implement fresh viable ideas quickly while needs are at their greatest.

It is interesting at this point to compare these Northern Irish developments with the English probation services. The latter are run by committees made up of lay magistrates from a local area. Therefore the magistrates in a sense are the employers of the probation officers. However these committees do not have clear policy-making powers, which remain in the hands of the Home Office in conjunction with the Chief probation officers. Recently there was a review of the structure of the probation service in England and Wales, with options under consideration including a central national service, referral boards akin to the Northern Irish Area Boards, or retaining the status quo. Following a vigorous campaign by the magistrates to avoid change, the basic structure remains unchanged, with some movement towards reduction in the number of committees, amalgamation of smaller areas, and widening of the membership of the local committees. Their budgets are provided on the basis of 20% from the local authority and 80% from the Home Office. In contrast, it was decided by the Lord Chief Justice in Northern Ireland that there should be no legal representation on the Board from the sentencers — the magistrates and judges. On the positive side, this means that there is no possibility of any incestuous collusion. As a result the Northern Irish probation officers meet with the Lord Chief Justice, the magistrates and judges as a separate organization; the sentencers are not their employers. The probation officers provide a service and in theory the Probation Board has the right to withdraw that service if circumstances dictate.

In terms of the training of the probation staff, the Service has thrived over the last ten years. Whereas there were approximately forty trainees in the Service, and a great number undertaking professional training in 1980, there are now about 116 probation officers, all of whom are professionally qualified. The majority of the officers are under 40 years of age and there is an even balance both in terms of gender and religion. Administratively the division of work has not fundamentally changed. Alongside the prison welfare teams, many of the probation officers, both in urban and rural areas carry "generalist" caseloads. In geographical "patches", a senior probation officer might act as the "Area Manager" for a group of five to ten staff. In addition there are some specialist teams, such as those involved in community service, day centres, art therapy, and clinical psychology. An interesting development has been the formation of a specialist team called "Prison Link" which works alongside the Northern Irish Association for the Care and Resettlement of Offenders (NIACRO) providing a range of services to prisoners' families and released prisoners themselves.

Overall the organizational chart translates into a fairly flat pyramid:

1	Chief Probation Officer (CPO)
1	Deputy Chief Probation Officer (DCPO)
5	Assistant Chief Probation Officers (ACPOs)
25	Senior Probation Officers
116	Probation Officers
	c. 100 Probation Assistants (non-CQSW)

Corporate strategies are worked out for a two year period and the ACPOs work with the DCPO and CPO as the senior management team. Their roles can be changed, ranging from functional, regional, specialist or project responsibilities. In developing the policies, they facilitate the work of the senior probation officers and their own area groups. Responsibility for the delivery of area services is devolved to the SPO or area manager. It has been decided that there will be more concentration on raising the level of service in certain regions over the next couple of years and ACPOs will have responsibility for particular geographical areas. The CPO relies on her Deputy to take responsibility for much of the inward management of the Service, whereas she concentrates on working with all the outside social systems which impact on the Service.

Major changes have taken place in the balance between incarceration and community care for adult offenders over the past decade. Whereas in 1980, the officers would have been working with a majority of very minor offenders, they have now in a sense moved up the tariffs, so that most of the adults under supervision have been in prison before including some very serious scheduled offenders. Interestingly, this shift in emphasis has actually helped the morale of the staff who enjoy the challenge of using their skills in the "deep end" of the work.

No doubt the morale has also been enhanced by the introduction of an organizational development plan with the emphasis on management by objectives. After lengthy debates about the methods of quantifying the services, there is now an agreed aid to help reduce offending. Tangible results include a whole team of probation officers working on the creation of employment opportunities for serious offenders, with the financial assistance of the Department of Economic Development. Negotiations have also been taking place for the creation of a specialist sex offenders' centre, as an extension to the existing practice, and a means of developing greater in-depth skills in working in this area.

Teams are encouraged to set objectives and measure performance with the help of research consultants. Obviously one key issue for quantification is the re-offending rate of people once they have finished their period of probation. But this is not straightforward information to obtain since, for instance, the police can only provide such information for the purpose of social inquiry reports. Furthermore criminal justice statistics, when published, are often already a year out of date. Nonetheless, the senior managers are now continually looking for ways of measuring the effectiveness of the service.

The Prison Role

Of central significance to the probation service has been the changing pattern in the Northern Ireland prison population. In 1969 there were 700—800 prisoners, most of them imprisoned for "ordinary" offences. By the early 1980s, the number of prisoners had risen to about 3,500, and the vast majority of these people were incarcerated for paramilitary or terrorist activities. In 1991, the population in prison has decreased to just under 1,500, of whom 400 are on remand. Of these people, 500—600 have been sentenced for terrorist or paramilitary offences. In fact, the "ordinary" crime rate is the lowest in the United Kingdom and the rate is not growing at anything like the level of England and Wales — the rates are diverging. For instance, Northumberland which is about the same geographical size and population as Northern Ireland experiences three times the number of indictable offences.

This rise and decline in numbers is reflected in a noteworthy way in the individual prisons. Belfast prison, at the height, was holding nearly 1,000 people and now about half that number are within its walls. Included in its population are remand prisoners and long-term prisoners who were not involved in paramilitary offences, such as sex offenders. Similarly the Maze Prison was declined from its peak of 1,500 offenders to a population of less than 500. Apart from a small number of "ordinary" prisoners, used as cleaners or aides, the bulk of this population is long-term paramilitary prisoners. The former Maze Compound where "special category" lifestyles were once permitted (akin to a prisoner-of-war camp) now has a mere eight or nine prisoners. In contrast Magheraberry is a prison for males and females, used primarily for long-term or life sentence prisoners who opt out of paramilitary control. At one stage the female population had dwindled to eight, but has risen recently following a spate of arrests of women for paramilitary offences. There are currently about 300 prisoners overall in the prison. In addition there is Magilligan Prison, used for long-term prisoners usually coming towards the end of their sentences, many of whom are "ordinary" offenders.

With regard to the Young Offenders' Centre, there were over 300 sentenced young offenders at one stage, but the population is now under 100. Partly this reflects the way in which the probation service has been effectively intervening as an alternative to custody. On the caseloads of the officers now are young people who in the past would have been serving sentences of anything up to 4 years. On the whole there is a large increase in the Court decisions facilitating this work, although in some areas, the innovations are sparse because of the attitudes of the local magistrates. This inconsistency also applies to Crown Court judges. Exacerbating this situation is the fact that since the 1980s the Court Service now comes under the Lord Chancellor's Office.

Juvenile Offenders

Reverting to the issue of residential care and custody for juveniles, the current situation is as follows:

the former girls' Training School at Whiteabbey has now been amalgamated with the boys' school, Rathgael, with the result that one centre at Bangor now caters for Protestant juvenile offenders both male and female. St Joseph's, Middletown, remains as a female centre, but is now predominantly populated by female young persons in need of care and protection. Although the number of juveniles overall in the Training Schools has diminished, there are still proportionately more than there should be if set alongside the reduction in juveniles coming before the Courts. Alongside the custodial institutions, however, the two centres at Ramoan (Save the Children Fund) and Runkerry (the Portcamon Project) are being used successfully as residential centres under the Fourth Condition of the Probation Order. Other novel interpretations of this Fourth Condition include literacy classes, summer activity schemes, horse husbandry courses, courses to teach fishing skills, and art therapy classes.

Probation and the Voluntary Sector

The probation service continues to have close liaison with EXTERN, NIACRO, and "Save the Children Fund". EXTERN runs workshops for adult offenders, hostels and a range of other activities; NIACRO specializes in support services for prisoners' families; and as indicated earlier "Save the Children Fund" owns the Ramoan Centre and seconds some of its staff to work with the probation service. In addition the probation service tried to encourage the participation of community organizations and funds some to undertake various projects. Some prefer not to be regarded as part of a formal Fourth Condition. For instance a leisure centre is funded to run specific courses for probation clients. Much broader than individual casework, probation work now tries to help create some sort of positive experience in a wide sense for the probation service, and this is seen as a potent means of reducing recidivism. It has been suggested that, while some efforts have been made to evaluate the effectiveness of such work, insufficient progress has been made in developing a theoretical frame of reference for the education and training of future professional staff. There may thus be a gap between actual practice and the content of social work training courses. Indeed it is argued that qualified youth and community workers are in practice better equipped to join Probation's ranks than CQSW graduates.

Nowadays, the vast majority of juvenile offences concern stolen property, car theft and associated offences. A much smaller number involve serious violence against the person.

A Service for People

TABLE 27 : - Juvenile Offenders 1980 - 1990

	1980	1981	1982	1983	1984	1985	1986	1987	1988	1989	1990
A	3,857	3,736	4,325	4,317	4,191	4,587	3,930	2,354	2,839	3,208	3,264
B	2,397	2,908	2,440	2,865	2,992	3,460	2,796	2,767	2,389	2,055	2,058
C	2,225	2,416	2,513	2,277	2,086	2,138	2,156	1,895	1,749	1,404	1,373
D	485	661	692	1,085	1,098	986	1,049	885	998	1,057	1,222

A   Potential offenders dealt with by way of juvenile warning and advice
B   Cases dealt with by way of official caution
C   Cases dealt with by way of prosecution
D   Cases in which no further action was taken

Sources: Chief Constable's Annual Report 1980-1990 Police Authority for Northern Ireland [18]

Once the young person appears in Court, and is perhaps committed to Training School, the probation service, in the absence of any legislative authority, will lose contact. After Training School, the young person comes out on Licence into the community supervised by a member of the Training School staff. This dichotomy is not in any sense reflecting an unwillingness on the part of the Training Schools to co-operate — it is a legislative requirement, but in professional terms it does not make sense. A small number of Training School staff are obliged to traverse the entire Province with the results that, not only is there no continuity in the professional relationship with the young person, but the after-care of necessity is relatively superficial. Unfortunately, too high a proportion of these young people end up quickly in the Young Offenders' Centre. If ever there was a need for instating a proper "continuum of care" then this is it!

With regard to the Lisnevin residential unit, this does not appear to have changed its actual function very fundamentally. Basically it still takes over the custody of male young persons who are deemed by Rathgael and St Patrick's to be beyond their control. The majority of the young people are referred by St Patrick's, an "old-fashioned" Training School still run by religious Brothers. Many of the inmates of St Patrick's have home addresses in West Belfast and, on absconding, can literally be home within five minutes. When patience has been exhausted, the staff of St Patrick's have them committed to Lisnevin, twenty miles down the Ards Peninsula. In essence, Lisnevin is used for the persistent absconder who is deemed unmanageable in an open environment. The notion of a secure custodial unit for juveniles was floated in the Black Report and Lisnevin, in effect, has adopted this role. In contrast, the ideal role for Lisnevin would be a place where the best resources are centred, where skilled staff devote all their attention to the needs of young people with very difficult entrenched problems. But in actuality it does not match this ideal. Its management committee is made up of staff from the other Training Schools. And its practices seem to have emanated from the inclinations of individuals rather than any coherent policy. The NIO does not appear to have involved itself in any depth. In effect practice at Lisnevin has reflected the 1980s as a period when change has depended on individuals as opposed to systems, or legislation, or policy.

Purchasers and Providers

The probation service adopts the attitude that the voluntary sector can actually do certain tasks more effectively. In practice, they can act quickly; they can work "in the client time zone"; and they can be imaginative and creative. They are not as tied to legislative concerns or bureaucratic procedures. Hence, through the purchasing of voluntary services, the size of the formal statutory service has been maintained at a controlled level. In addition there is a philosophical issue as to whether communities should be encouraged to deal with their own problems of crime. This is to be carefully distinguished from the role of the professional officer, as an accountable public servant, who makes recommendations to a court of law which may determine whether or not a person's actual liberty is affected. Such statutory obligations carried out by a probation officer could never be attributed to voluntary community groups, as this would place them in an impossible dilemma even if it were objectively feasible!

It is fallacious to assume that the purchasing of services from voluntary organizations is always a cheap option. Sometimes their unit of resource may be cheaper because of the very fact that they are not part of large bureaucracies. But a danger inherent in this type of partnership in the sense that the voluntary organizations can begin to imitate the statutory agencies, employing professional staff and in the process losing their innovatory creativity. If this happens they stop being representatives of the community. It is also important that the nature of the relationship is clearly recognized. Statutory organizations must remain the senior partners who ultimately retain the responsibility for the quality of the services delivered. Especially in the instance where an offender is carrying out activities in the community in an entrusted way, it will be the probation service which attracts the opprobrium if the experiment goes drastically wrong, more so than the voluntary agency. Another vital element in the relationship is the fact that the probation service may try other alternatives if Community Service fails, such as a day centre programme, before bringing the person back to Court as in breach of an Order. Community Service may not be the only resort but the professional officers have to remain the arbiters in such decision-making.

The Autonomy of the Probation Service

It is crucially important that the probation service is perceived to be independent and professionally neutral. In contrast, it is probably fair to say that the general public is very unclear about the functioning of the Statutory Social Services Boards. There are too many contradictory messages between management and workers, between caring roles and controlling roles. In Probation, although there are elements of control, the client usually has clearly defined rights. For instance, if taken to Court on a Breach of a Probation Order, a client can hire a Queens Counsel on legal aid to dispute the action. In contrast parents whose children have been committed to Care under the Care and Protection legislation have to find ways of combatting the vaguer assertion that the legal actions were taken "in the best interests" of the children.

Probation and Paramilitaries

The Service faced a situation from the 1970s onwards where the prison population was increasing but the majority of the inmates did not see themselves as offenders; they saw themselves as political prisoners. Articulate, intelligent and angry people, they in a sense challenged Probation to offer a relevant service, and this led to a form of negotiation. The probation service as a result had to clarify its role. For instance they had to cope with the fact that in the early 1980s, they were not allowed access to prisoners individually, but had to work through a "spokesman". On the grounds that social work practice was based on the principle of individualization of the person, the probation service eventually refused to work on the spokesman basis. After a hiatus of about a year and a half during which all communication ceased with Provisional IRA prisoners, access was restored to individual prisoners, at their own request. One of the accepted conditions was that prisoners had a right to see their files. As a result, it made the probation officers sharpen up their own thinking about the nature of record-keeping; what is relevant to objectives; what is factual or what is conjecture.

Furthermore it was decided that, consistent with offering services on a consumer basis, a newspaper should be specially printed as a way of giving prisoners and their families information. This was a valid means of providing a relevant service in accord with professional principles and the demands of the client group. In fact there are now aspects of the Northern Irish probation service which are a decade in advance of their counterparts in England and Wales. At the outset, paramilitary prisoners viewed their own "welfare" organizations as superior to and more effective than the probation service. But the service maintained a consistent stance as paid agents of the State who would not collude with law-breaking. Eventually prisoners and their outside representatives recognized the professionalism of the service, the strengths in *not* being members of the community, the importance of the ethic of confidentiality; and the ability to negotiate within and between formal systems. In return the probation service has been compelled to help prisoners from their own point of view, not enforcing professional prescriptions externally. The demanding articulate group of prisoners in Northern Irish prisons has been in stark contrast to prisoners in England and Wales who are seen and behave as powerless and brutalized individuals. This mutual learning in the Northern Irish service has reinforced a key truth for social work practice, that power and authority have to be shared, equalized in order to achieve real breakthrough. Otherwise it is simply ideological domination, however subtle or crude. But it has also taken tremendous courage on the part of the senior officers of the service. For instance Loyalist paramilitaries were actually confronted about the futility of punishment shootings, and this led to the present situation, where young offenders are ordered by the paramilitaries to turn up for their Probation appointments.

In spite of the continued avowal by Sinn Fein that West Belfast Catholic communities have to be protected from ordinary criminals by paramilitaries (and persuasive arguments are used that this is really preventing anarchy), there is a growing recognition that even in any ideal future world which they envisage, their communities will need some form of professional social work service. It is a tribute to the current probation service that they have been accepted across the whole political and religious spectrum in Northern Ireland as providing a reliable, trustworthy and beneficial service.[19]

CHAPTER V
References

1 *Strategy for the Development of Health and Personal Social Services in Northern Ireland*, (1975), HMSO.
2 "Past 65. Who Cares?"
3 "The Way Forward".
4 Review of Mental Handicap Services.
5 *Homes and Hostels for Children and Young People*, (June 1982). DHSS (NI) (Sheridan Report). HMSO.
6 DHSS (NI) (1986), *Report of the Committee of Enquiry into Children's Homes and Hostels*, (Hughes Report). HMSO.
7 Pinkerton J & Kelly G (1986) "Kincora Affair - the Aftermath", *Youth and Policy* No 17, pps 22/23.
8 Lynch J (28th - 30th September 1986) "A footnote to Kincora - from the detection of abuses to the abuses of detection", Second North-South Child Welfare Conference. Pinkerton J (ed), *Child Care in Crisis - What can we create?* pps. 16/17.
9 op cit p.24
10 Sone K (9th May 1991) "Under New Management", *Community Care*, pps 12/13.
11 op cit p.13
12 Challis D et al (1989-90)
"Assessment and case management", *Social Work and Social Science Review*, 1 (3), pp 147 – 162.
13 Department of Health (1989), *Caring for People*, HMSO.
14 Department of Health and Social Services, Northern Ireland. (1990) "People First", HMSO.
15 Department of Health and Social Services (1979), *Psychiatric Hospitals in Northern Ireland*, HMSO.
16 Hall J and Gibson M (1988),
Short- term support for elderly people discharged from hospital.
Personal Social Services in Northern Ireland, DHSS.
17 Reid G (1991), *The North Belfast Dementia Project.*
Personal Social Services in Northern Ireland, DHSS.
18 *Chief Constable's Annual Reports 1980-90*, Police Authority for Northern Ireland.
19 The authors acknowledge their indebtedness to Mrs Breidge Gadd, Chief Probation Officer for Northern Ireland, for her substantial contribution of descriptive material for this chapter through taped interview.

Chapter V
Summary of Legislation 1980-90

1982	Probation Board (NI) Order
1986	Mental Health (NI) Order
1987	Adoption (NI) Order
1990	Diabled Persons (NI) Act

CHAPTER VI
The Need for Community Self - Determination

Reflections on the Demise of Professional Social Work

This book has represented an absorbing historical journey. Along the route, we have witnessed how the English Poor Law was superimposed on an Ireland, North and South, in an ill-fitting but remorseless manner. As positive responses to gross deprivation towards the end of the nineteenth century, various voluntary organizations strove to bring succour and tangible assistance to the disenfranchised poor. Eventually the Poor Law was dismantled, and as a side benefit of the political union with Britain after 1921, Northern Ireland received step by step the social legislation and statutory services that were to comprise the "Welfare State". Professional training and clearly delineated statutory duties led to the growth of efficient and client-centred welfare authorities and the probation service. Efforts by the statutory agencies to replace the old edifices and assumptions of the Poor Law were ably supported by resilient voluntary organizations whose pioneering zeal enriched the personal social services. When the restructuring of services into corporate health and social services Boards happened in 1972, it was hoped that social needs would be met in an even more organized and forward-looking way through integrated "programmes of care". However, with a few notable exceptions, this key concept appeared to be smothered at birth by a plethora of bureaucratic structures. Further depersonalisation of the social services was to follow with the introduction of general managers at central and district levels who added to the bureaucratic congestion and created more managerial jargon to justify their existence and mystify the already bemused consumers of the services. It is no coincidence that the probation service has, in contrast, remained clearly focused on its primary objectives. Unlike the four largely non-accountable Area Boards for Health and personal social services, two thirds of whose committee members are still nominated, the probation service reports to a single Board and has a relatively simple local office structure. It also seems to facilitate much more in its career structure those probation officers who wish to remain in direct practice in the community. Even in the Probation Board, however, there are indications of the dangers inherent in a top tier management committee of individual nominees who tend to be the passive agents for transmitted government dictate.

One of the saddest features of the demise of statutory social work has been the manner in which trained social work practitioners have continually been sucked into middle management positions, detached from the local communities, and ill-equipped to carry out their ambiguous functions. It is an era in which we are witnessing a total displacement of goals away from the clear visions of meeting social needs which were manifest in the immediate post-war period. The latter-day managerial encumbents of the statutory personal social services appear to have unconsciously accepted and rationalized a new goal — to make sure that the large complex mechanistic bureaucracy is and remains self-perpetuating. As indicated earlier, the main consumer-centred innovations are emanating from the voluntary organizations. And ironically it is as if the wheel has turned full circle. In keeping with the current political ideology, the managers of the statutory Boards are now beginning to interpret their roles as services "purchasers", not service "providers". In effect they will be inviting increasingly the voluntary organizations to bid for contracts to provide the services deemed to be necessary for the various areas. And the contracts will be awarded to those organizations who can produce the services for the least cost. Already struggling to cover what they perceive as gaps in statutory provision with their limited resources, including unpaid volunteers in many instances, the voluntary organizations find themselves in an unwanted competitive, even cut-throat situation. One inevitable conclusion arising from this narrative history is that the caring professions have spawned an array of managerial "Emperors with no clothes" whose credentials need to be re-examined.

Northern Ireland is a precarious little country, having an uncertain political link with Britain and a high incidence of social need. It has no self-government in the sense that district councils are now only emasculated forums looking after dust-bin collection and rat catching. Overviewing the policies in relation to education, health and social services, the Area Boards act in effect as the passive agents of the respective British Government departments. Northern Irish society is riddled with conflict, generations old, and the very legitimacy of its existence is questioned both through some democratically elected representatives and paramilitary violence. Perhaps the highly centralized and controlling hierarchy which has emerged in the statutory health and social services is a manifestation of this state of affairs. Could it be that these managerial agents of the DHSS are in fact constituent parts of a coping mechanism to ward off moral panic about possible societal collapse? It is perhaps not so strange that there has been little advancement in democratic community care if there are really profound and covert fears about the erosion of the very social fabric. Social work appears to have moved away completely and effectively from its key principles of self-determination and personal autonomy and become incorporated in the state machinery of social control. Moreover, in order to maintain this function its managers are now employed, not to help individuals and communities to achieve self-determination, but to keep them at arm's length.

The Challenge for Social Work Education

Arising from this dismal scenario are several unavoidable challenges for the social work educators. Throughout this text, reference has been made to the dearth of relevant qualifications among residential and day care workers. If the great issues of the next century are to be addressed, including the securing of a quality of life for the growing proportion of very elderly people or those significantly disabled, then a coherent training programme must be developed urgently. The framework provided by the National Council for Vocational Qualifications (set up in 1985) seems to offer a flexible way forward, based on partnership between employers, trade unions and institutions of further and higher education. Essentially the aim is to set standards which are applicable to the different branches of caring work, establishing the requisite knowledge and skills. Forms of assessment include a direct observation, simulated exercises, and written assignments. Most of these assessments are envisaged as being carried out by line managers and supervisors, who themselves will require training and assessment skills. If this accumulation of credits in "modules" of competence proves to be feasible, it will lead to greater transferability of qualified employees between related occupations. It would appear that the NVQ will serve to improve the skills of caring workers such as day care and residential assistants, and this could signify an improvement in the quality of work with some of the most vulnerable of the clientele of the social services — those dependent on physical and emotional care because of their age, disability or deprivation.[1]

However this is only part of a much wider transformation required in social work education. As indicated earlier in this text, CQSW education and training has been strongly criticized because of its lack of direction, fragmentation and limited traditional focus. For instance, the lack of specific and intensive training in group and community work in Northern Irish CQSW courses has caused the criticism that it is an inadequate preparation for the probation service, the focus of which is increasingly on family and group work.

It is to be hoped that the national policy changes concerning CQSW education and training will have positive consequences for Northern Ireland. In 1989 the Central Council for Education and Training in Social Work gave its assent to a new comprehensive award, the Diploma in Social Work, and set a deadline for completion of its introduction by 1994/95. In practice this will be the universally recognized qualification for social workers and probation officers in all settings. Requiring a minimum of two years study and supervised practice at the level of higher education, courses will have to embody content relating to knowledge, skills and values which reflects a national standard. A central feature will be the close working collaboration between educational institutions and the programme providers, the practice agencies. Former courses leading to Certificates in social services will be converted with the aid of Government developments. It is envisaged that a progressive framework for education and training in social work and social care, that is, the full range of the personal social services, will be developed.

Clearly responding to the calls for greater applied relevance to employers, CCETSW states that only Diploma in Social Work programmes submitted by "programme providers" will be considered. Programme providers are defined as "an educational institution or institutions together with a social services agency or agencies providing a programme leading to the award of the Certificate." [2] Reinforcing the integration of theory and practice, CCETSW requires that a period of at least six months (including at least 80 days) must be spent in practice in the final stage of the programme, and the students must be supervised by accredited practice teachers in approved agencies. Consistency in assessment and provision of learning opportunities will be enhanced by Practice Assessment Panels and Programme Assessment Boards.

The basic philosophy of the Dip SW is founded on the belief that, whatever the setting of the practitioner, all social workers share a common core of knowledge, skills and values. In this respect, the expected content of the courses mirrors very closely the theoretical frameworks developed in the 1970s which described the generic common base of practice or experimented with social systems approaches. However there is a refreshing determination within all CCETSW pronouncements to encourage innovation, flexibility and variety in approach. [3,4,5]

Furthermore, in the spirit that consumers of personal social services have the right to expect the best possible standards, CCETSW has been keen to promote a continuum of post-qualifying professional development opportunities for social care and social work staff. This framework will have six components.

— a credit accumulation and transfer system (CATS) linked to academic awards;
— post qualifying and advanced levels of professional development leading to CCETSW's Advanced Award;
— assessment of learning outcomes;

— implementation through consortia of agencies and educational institutions;
— a monitoring system; and
— a UK-wide standard of education and training established and maintained by CCETSW. [6]

The positive intent to implement the six year plan in Northern Ireland was specifically outlined in May 1990, with the following targets set for 1994/95:

— a programme of conversions to DipSW programmes (largely involving Queen's University Belfast and the University of Ulster);
— the recognition of 160 accredited practice teachers. [7]

The determination of CCETSW to prepare a structure of education and training relevant to the social needs of the next century is indeed laudable. It is crucially important however that the right balance is achieved between applied relevance (how to do the job at hand) and critical ability (asking the question "why "). It is one of the very sad features of the decline of social work practice in Northern Ireland that ossified complex organizations have been allowed to displace the original goals of professional social work with a totally unjustifiable detachment from local communities. A social services agency only retains its validity if it can justify its original functions (and answer the question "why ?"). Perhaps the new breeds of qualified social workers will be more alert to the dangers of self-perpetuating meritocracy. However there is also a responsibility on the part of the senior management in the personal social services to provide a career structure which recognizes tangibly outstanding social work practice, and diminishes the likelihood of administrative flight from the client consumers.

Direct Rule and its Consequences in Terms of Social Policy

"You do not have to be unemployed in Northern Ireland today to experience poverty; some informants point out that although they were working they still could not cope, simply because they were in low-paid jobs. This is called the poverty-trap, and it perpetuates the vicious circle, especially when the higher cost of living in Northern Ireland is taken into consideration. Being out of work or being in a low-paid job was the economic reality for so many of the informants interviewed... " [8]

In a study based on recorded interviews with working-class people in Northern Ireland, "men and women, young and old, of all religions and of none", McNamee and Lovett sought to convey what they thought about subjects vital to themselves in their every day life. In the course of their investigations, they confirmed that vandalism is a massive problem in the post-war housing estates throughout the Province; women are continually treated as "poor relations and second-class social citizens"; there is a severe lack of adequate child care facilities, related both to absence of funding and indifferent attitudes among the authorities; the 'Troubles' (ie paramilitary violence) visits death and destruction disproportionately on to working-class people in their own areas and communities.[9]

Giving additional confirmation of the plight of low income groups, Child Care Northern Ireland recently published the following bleak statistics:

27 in every 100 children in Northern Ireland live in families dependent on income support;

more than 95,000 children live in single parent families;

children under 4 years of age are 35% less likely to attend playgroup facilities than those in the rest of the United Kingdom;

from October 1990 to September 1991, 7,771 children were the dependants of families who approached the Housing Executive because they had nowhere to live.[10]

Alongside these social realities there has been a tangible groundswell of opinion that the positive potential for social change within communities throughout Northern Ireland can be tapped if only the right mechanisms can be worked out. In other words, the means has to be achieved to enable working-class communities, Catholic and Protestant, to enter into a dialectic and find the courage to sustain it until a new form of society emerges.

When these pious hopes are placed alongside the actual "official" machinery in relation to social policy, the contours of social reality are somewhat different. Apart from the notable exception of the probation service, the modern function of statutory social services appears to be maintenance of social stability and control at the most economical costs. Far from energizing and empowering local communities, these management structures are more consistent with the general "Direct Rule" ethos of "keeping the lid on the Ulster problem". With such a concentrated focus on security issues, it is hardly surprising that there has been no coherent statutory response to the recommendation of the Black Committee in relation to juvenile offenders. It would also seem to be the case that the new "Child Care Order" will be more a tidying up exercise regarding the general care and protection of children than a flagship for fundamental change. In the face of a growing population of aged and infirm people, the reliance on market forces has allowed an array of private nursing homes of varying quality to assume the mantle of responsibility for the major social issue of the next century. Where the greatest impact has occurred in terms of enlightened policy, and mental health and mental handicap services are examples, the vibrancy of some voluntary organizations in keeping these special needs to the fore has had a significant role.

Community Empowerment

There is a general inadequacy in defining the needs of citizens of the Northern Ireland population who are most at risk. Most of these people are born into and live among the working-class populations in the Province. It is here that the greatest incidences of unemployment, poverty, poor housing, lack of social facilities, and general demoralization, occur. Their needs transcend any debate about political and religious differences. Such "differences" are artificial constructs which in effect serve to separate individuals and families who experience common human needs. Tragically "Direct Rule" by its very nature fails to facilitate the merging of these people's interests. In stark contrast, security policies seem intent on maintaining a "stand-off", under military control.

Potentially professional social work practice should be capable of exercising a tremendous influence on social change in these circumstances. For social work principles in their pure form have to do with empowerment, local self-determination and regaining autonomy. Whether it is work with the individual or family or larger group, a basic tenet in social work is that the agenda for change must be established by the participants so that they can be committed to and give their energy to this process. It also takes courage in the sense that it is not possible to predetermine the outcome of a process of change, but it is important to maintain a faith that the eventual results of efforts will be positive. The collective efforts of ordinary people where all have originally agreed to work for a better future, **will** produce positive results.

To suggest that such a process can take place only in the realm of social services policy would be of course futile. There must be many strands of commitment. A transformation in the structure of the educational system is also imperative, so that children and young people can literally physically be accessible to each other to engage in the de-mythologizing of centuries of conditioning. But there is no doubt that the first profound steps to move from Direct Rule to empowerment must be taken by local people in local communities. And the future structure of the social services must be geared to facilitate this. Otherwise, if the present trend continued towards more and more detached managerialism, then the official structures will really be nothing more than controlling mechanisms of a confused colonial administration, stumbling myopically into the twenty first century.

CHAPTER VI
References

1. Smyth T (27 July 1990), 'Testing Time to Qualify', *Care Weekly*.
2. *Rules and Requirements for the Diploma in Social Work*, CCETSW Paper 30, Second Edition 1991, p 22.
3. *Improving Standards in Practice Learning*, CCETSW Paper 26.3, August 1989.
4. *NVQ Guidance on Approval of Assessment Arrangements*, CCETSW Paper 29.1, December 1990.
5. *NVQ Requirements for Approval of Assessment Centres* and an *Award of Qualifications by CCETSW*, CCETSW Paper 29, December 1990.
6. *Continuing Professional Development for Staff of the Personal Social Services*, CCETSW Summary Paper 1991.
7. *The Requirements for Post Qualifying Education and Training in the personal social services - A Framework for Continuing Professional Development*, CCETSW Paper 31, December 1990.
8. McNamee P & Lovett T (1987), *Working Class Community in Northern Ireland*, p 114, Ulster People's College.
9. Ibid.
10. *Child Care Northern Ireland*, (December 1991).

BIBLIOGRAPHY

Adoption Bill, Second Reading 1929, Northern Ireland House of Commons.
Allan, A and Morton, A (1961), *This is Your Child*, Routledge and Kegan Paul, London.
Anderson, T, *These Fifty Years-The Story of the North Belfast Mission*.
Annual Report 1924, Belfast Council of Social Welfare
Annual Report 1927, Belfast Council of Social Welfare
Annual Report 1929, Belfast Council of Social Welfare
Annual Reports of the Ministry of Health and Local Government.
Belfast Newsletter, 26 November 1936.
Beresford J O (1976), *Some considerations on the Amalgamation or otherwise of the Northern Ireland Probation and After-care Service into the Personal Social Services System in Northern Ireland*, Unpublished thesis, NUU Coleraine, November.
Brown, W D D (1968), 'Ye Olde Welfayre', *Contact Magazine*, Belfast Welfare Authority.
Budge, J and O'Leary C (1973), *Belfast - Approach to Crisis 1613-1970*, McMullan
Calvert, I Mrs, Northern Ireland House of Commons 1949, *Welfare Services Bill (Second Reading)*.
Census of Children in Care (June 1977), Department of Health and Social Services.
Challis D (1989-90), 'Assessment and Case Management', *Social Work and Social Science Review 1 (3)*, pp 147-162.
Chief Constable's Annual Reports 1980-90, Police Authority for Northern Ireland.
Child Care Northern Ireland, (December 1991).
Child Welfare Council (1954), *Interim Report on Juvenile Delinquency*, HMSO.
Child Welfare Council (1956), *Children in Care*, HMSO.
Child Welfare Council (1960), *Operation of the Juvenile Courts in Northern Ireland*, HMSO.
Child Welfare Council (1960), *The Operation of the Social Services in relation to Child Welfare*, HMSO.
Child Welfare Council (1963), *Adoption of Children*, HMSO.
Child Welfare Council (1966), *The Role of the Voluntary Homes in the Child Care Service*, HMSO.
Child Welfare Council (1969), *Report on the Children and Young Persons Boarding-out Regulations*, HMSO.
Children (Amendment) Bill, Second Reading, Northern Ireland House of Commons.
Consultative Paper on the Structure and Managements of Health & Personal Social Services in Northern Ireland, (December 1979) DHSS, HMSO.
Continuing Professional Development for Staff of the Personal Social Services, (1991) CCETSW Summary Paper.
Darby, J & Williamson (eds) (1978), *Violence and the Social Services in Northern Ireland*, Heinemann. *Strategy for the Development of Health and Personal Social Services in Northern Ireland*, (1975) HMSO.
Department of Business Studies, Queen's University of Belfast, (first Report August 1974. Second Report April 1976), *The Reorganizations of Health and Personal Social Services in Northern Ireland*, Sponsored by the Nuffield Provincial Hospitals Trust.
Department of Health (1989), *Caring for People*, HMSO.
Department of Health and Social Services, Northern Ireland. (1990), *People First*, HMSO.

Department of Health and Social Services (1979), *Psychiatric Hospitals in Northern Ireland*, HMSO.

DHSS (NI) (1986), *Report of the Committee of Enquiry into Children's Homes and Hostels*, (Hughes Report). HMSO.

DHSS (NI) (June 1982), *Homes and Hostels for Children and Young People*, (Sheriden Report), HMSO.

Dolan, Breidge (May 1975), 'Community Service Orders - a History of the Scheme', *Quest - Journal No 3*.

Evason, E, Darby, J and Pearson, M (1976), *Social Need and Social Provision in Northern Ireland*, New University of Ulster, Coleraine.

Evason, Eileen (1978), 'Family Poverty in Northern Ireland', *Poverty Research Series No 6*, Child Poverty Action Group.

Farrell, Michael (1978), *The Poor Law and the Workhouse in Belfast 1834-1948*, Northern Ireland Public Records Office

Government and the Voluntary Sector (1978), HMSO.

Griffiths H, Ni Giolla Choille T, Robinson J (1978), *Yesterday's Heritage or Tomorrow's Resource*, NUU.

Hall J and Gibson M (1988), *Short-term support for elderly people discharged from hospital*, Personal Social Services in Northern Ireland, DHSS.

Hay J R, *The Development of the British Welfare State*.

Improving Standards in Practice Learning, (August 1989), CCETSW Paper 26.3.

Jamison, E R (1968) 'Ye Olde Welfayre', *Contact Magazine*, Belfast Welfare Authority.

Kelly, R McF, *The Roots of Rathgael*.

Lawrence, R J (1965), *The Government of Northern Ireland*, Clarendon Press Oxford

Lynch J (28th 30th September 1986), 'A footnote to Kincora—from the detection of abuses to the abuses of detection', Second North-South Child Welfare Conference.

MacBeath, A A, *Fifty Years of Social Work 1906-1956—a brief history of the work of Belfast Council of Social Welfare*, Nicholson & Bass

Malcolm, A G (1851), *The History of the General Hospital, Belfast and the other medical institutions of the town*, Belfast.

McCormac H (1853), *Moral Sanatory Economy*, London. Report of the Commissioners of Inquiry into the Origin and Character of the Riots in Belfast in 1852. (1858), Cmnd 333, London.

McNamee P & Lovett T (1987), *Working Class Community in Northern Ireland*, Ulster People's College, p 114.

Mental Treatment Bill, Second Reading, 1932, Northern Ireland House of Commons.

Much of the above material is based on John Beresford's unpublished thesis (November 1976) *Some considerations on the Amalgamation or otherwise of the Northern Ireland Probation and After-care Service into the Personal Social Services system in Northern Ireland*, NUU, Coleraine.

Newe, B G (1963), *The story of the Northern Ireland Council of Social Service 1938-1963*, NICSS.

Nicholls, G (1853), *A History of the Irish Poor Law*, John Murray, London.

Northern Whig, 6 May 1936

NVQ Guidance on Approval of Assessment Arrangements (December 1990), CCETSW Paper 29.1.

NVQ Requirements for Approval of Assessment Centres and an Award of Qualifications by CCETSW, (December 1990) CCETSW Paper 29.

Official opening of St Patrick's Training School on 10 September 1957 commemoration booklet.

Oliver, J A (1978), *Working at Stormont*, Dublin Institute of Public Administration.

Paor, Liam de (1969), *Divided Ulster*, Penguin

Papers relating to proceedings for the relief of distress in Ireland. Fourth series. (1847) HMSO, London.

'*Past 65. Who Cares?*'

Personal Communication from Miss M E Hall, former Principal Social Worker (Health Care), Eastern Health & Social Services Board.

Pinkerton J (ed) *Child Care in Crisis —What can we create?* pps. 16/17 and p. 24

Pinkerton J & Kelly G (1986) 'Kincora Affair—the Aftermath', *Youth and Policy No 17*, pps 22/23.

Progress in Ulster since 1921, Town and Country Development Committee, Northern Ireland Council of Social Service

Reid G (1991), *The North Belfast Dementia Project*, Personal Social Services in Northern Ireland, DHSS.

Report of the Belfast Riots, Commissioners (1887), Cmnd 4925, HMSO, London.

Report of the Committee on the Protection and Welfare of the Young and the Treatment of Young Offenders, (1938) Cmnd 187.

Report of the Departmental Commission on Local Government Administration ,1927, Cmnd 73

Report of the Departmental Committee on the number and character of committals to Reformatory and Industrial Schools and provision of a Borstal, 1923, Cmnd 14.

Report of the Vice-regal Commisson on Poor Law Reform in Ireland, (1906) Cmnd 3202, HMSO, London.

Report on Services for Hearing Impaired People, (March 1977) Central Personal Social Services for Blind, Partially Sighted and Hearing Impaired People.

Report on the Administration of Local Government Services, 1928/29. Cmnd 110

Residential Staff Census, (November 1975) Northern Ireland Residential Social Work Liaison Group.

Review of Mental Handicap Services.

Royal Commission on the Poor Laws and Relief of Distress; Report on Ireland, (1909) Cmnd 4630. HMSO, London.

Rules and Requirements for the Diploma in Social Work, (1991) CCETSW Paper 30, Second Edition p 22.

Seed, P (1973), *The Expansion of Social Work in Britain*, Routledge & Kegan Paul.

Seventh Annual Report, Belfast Council of Social Welfare (1922).

Smyth T (27 July 1990), 'Testing Time to Qualify', *Care Weekly*.

Sone K (9th May 1991), 'Under New Management', *Community Care*, pps 12/13.

Stratety for the Development of Health and Personal Social Services in Northern Ireland, (1975), HMSO.

The Protection and Welfare of Young and the Treatment of the Young Offender, (1946), Government White Paper, Cmnd 264, HMSO.

The Requirements for Post Qualifying Education and Training in the Personal Social Services— A Framework for Continuing Professional Development, (December 1990) CCETSW, Paper 31.
The Way Forward
Townsend, Meryl (1977), *The Need for Care*, Social Work Advisory Group DHSS.
Woodham-Smith, C (1968), *The Great Hunger*, Hamish Hamilton, London.

A one-roomed cabin on a beach near Larne, Co Antrim, similar to a great number of dwellings in use before the Irish Famine.
(From the R J Welch Collection; reproduced by kind permission of the Ulster Museum)

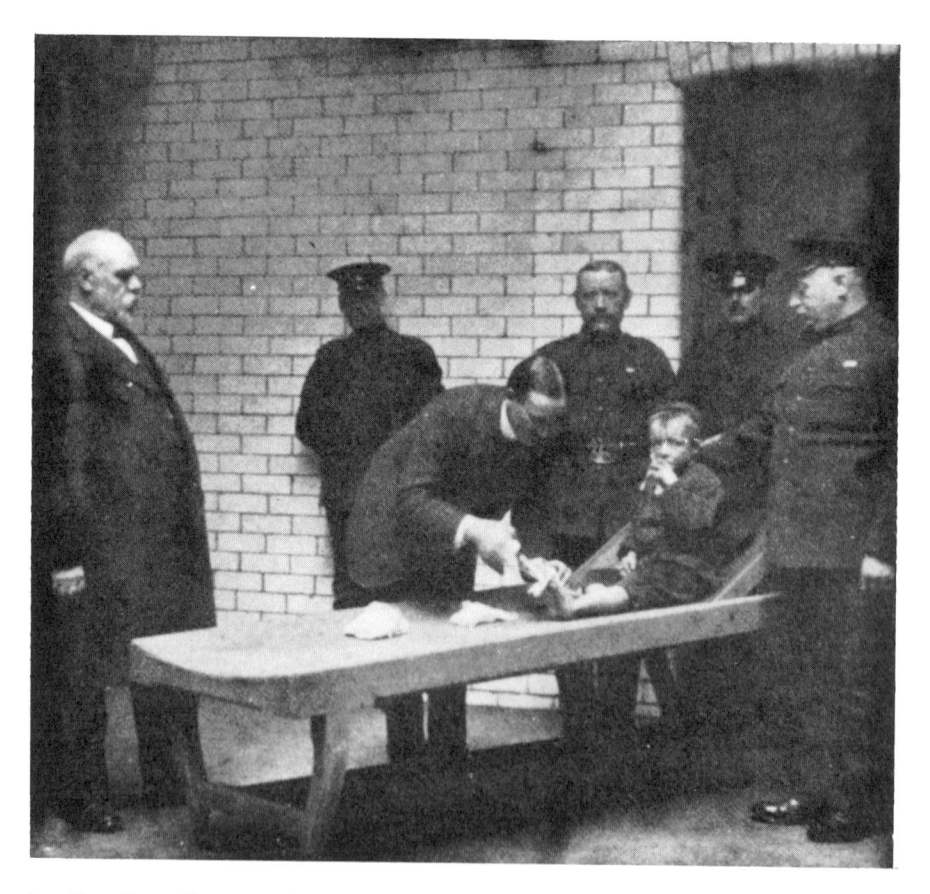

A police Court Surgeon gives medical treatment to a vagrant child, while the Court Missionary looks on (1909).
(Reproduced from the D J Hogg Collection by kind permission of Linenhall Library.)

The Court Missionary at Belfast police court supervises a young man who is signing a Temperance Pledge (1909). The Court Missionaries were the forerunners of the modern probation service.
(Reproduced from the D J Hogg Collection by kind permission of Linenhall Library.)

A dormitory in the Belfast Workhouse — note the raised floor on which straw palliasses were placed to serve as beds.
(Reproduced by kind permission of the Northern Ireland Public Records Office)

The facade of the Belfast Workhouse.
(Reproduced by kind permission of the Northern Ireland Public Records Office)

The Poor House and Infirmary opened by the Belfast Charitable Society in 1774. This building is still in existence in Clifton Street, Belfast, providing care for the elderly.
(Reproduced by kind permission of the Ulster Museum)

Muckamore House. Opened in 1949 in Co Antrim for the care of 'Mental Defectives'.
(Photograph by A Feenan)

'Lynwood' hostel for the mentally handicapped, opened in 1978 on the Ballyduff estate, Co Antrim, by the Northern Health and Social Services Board.
(Photograph by A Feenan)

Index

Act of Union, 1,3
Adoption, 17, 48, 77, 94, 142
Almoners: birth of the almoner service, 57; training and professional identity, 88; adoption of term 'medical social worker', 89

Barnardo's: origins, 21; work of 1899-1906, 22; children in Barnardo's care, 87
Belfast, growth of population, 10, 16
Belfast Charitable Society, 8
Belfast Council of Social Welfare, 25, 59, 64
Belfast Hospitals After-Care Committee, 57, 59
Black Committee, 123
Blind people, 14, 17, 57, 86
Board of Guardians, 6, 17, 72
Boarding-out regulations, 51, 76
Bridewell, 2

Central government, 40, 107
Charity Organisation Society, 24
Charter Schools, 2
Child care: baby farming, 50; boarding-out, 29, 51, 72, 94, 123; Child Welfare Councils, 73, 77, 96, 99; in workhouse, 27, 43, 74, 87; preventative, 97; voluntary, 13, 18, 28, 81, 87
Citizens' Advice Bureaux, 61
Community Relations, 15, 107
Court Missionaries, 21

Deaf people, 11, 17, 94
Demography, 10, 14, 42, 127
Disability services, 11, 86, 147
Dispensaries, 6, 16

Education and training for social work, 61, 73, 92, 101, 127, 165
Elderly people: in the workhouse, 26, 42; old people's homes, 84, 85, 126; services 1980-1990, 126, 135
Epidemics, 6, 11

Famine, 11, 14

Home Help service, 84, 85
Hospitals: fever, 3, 6, 27, 30; lying-in, 8, 28; voluntary, 44
House of Commons Committees, 3
House of Correction/Industry, 2
Housing, 4, 5, 10, 12, 42, 52

Industrial schools, 19, 47, 73, 74
Infirmaries, 2, 6
Insanity, 8, 55

Juvenile Courts: court or educational tribunal, 51; inadequate accommodation, 91; review of constitution and procedures, 67, 124
Juvenile delinquency, 19, 47, 52, 79

Kincora, 138

Local government, 8, 14, 17, 40, 42
Lunacy, 3, 4, 9, 55
Lynn committee, 50, 55

Maternity services, 8, 28, 62
Mental handicap, 63, 102, 112, 138
Mental health: 8, 9, 17, 28, 31, 33; framework, 79, 100, 137; services, 17, 55, 63, 80, 93
Municipal government, 8

page 183

NSPCC, 21, 102, 128
Nicholls, G, 1, 5
North Belfast Mission, 23
Northern Ireland Council of Social Service, 61

Offenders, 19
Outdoor relief, 6, 11, 13, 31, 43, 44, 45

Poor Law, 1, 4, 26, 45
Poverty, 23, 44, 58, 60, 121, 168
Probation: birth of, 21; Probation Officers in 1938, 54; paramilitaries and, 158; role of Court Missionaries, 21; structure of modern service, 150; training and staff development, 101

Reformatories: establishment of, 20; Report of Departmental Committee on Industrial Schools, 47
Relieving Officers, 7, 31, 72
Riots, 15, 46, 102

St Patrick's Training School, 19

'Sick', 2, 6, 16, 26, 27
Sisters of Nazareth, 18
Social conditions, 16, 41, 168

Training schools: introduction of the term, 47; role of 143; training school after-care, 156
Tuberculosis, 62

Unemployment, 41, 61

Violence: probation and, 158; social work and, 110; social work in 'The Troubles', 102
Victoria Homes, 19
Voluntary organisations: voluntary societies in the 19th century, 11

Welfare Authorities: expansion of services in 1960s, 82; formation of, 70; problems and achievements of, 92
Welfare State, 67
Workhouses: Dublin, 2; Cork, 2; places available, 7, 26, 42, 81

page 184